The Princes of Malta

The Grand Masters
of the Order of St John in Malta

1530-1798

CHARLES MULA

The Princes of Malta

The Grand Masters
of the Order of St John in Malta

1530-1798

Publishers Enterprises Group (PEG) Ltd

Published by
Publishers Enterprises Group (PEG) Ltd
P.E.G. Building, UB7 Industrial Estate, San Ġwann SGN 09
Malta

Web site: http.//www.peg.com.mt
E-mail: contact@peg.mt

First published 2000

ISBN: 99909-0-263-1

Photoset and printed in Malta by P.E.G. Ltd

TO

THE THREE WOMEN

IN OUR LIVES

NAMED *MARIA*

THIS WORK IS DEDICATED

Julia and Charles

Acknowledgements

Charles Mula and Publishers Enterprises Group (PEG) Ltd are indebted to Mr Louis J. Scerri for editing and proof-reading this book.

Thanks are also due to Mr Michael Galea for his assistance in the selection of, and for providing most of the photographs.

Contents

Preface

The Maltese archipelago consists of three inhabited islands. The largest, Malta, is approximately 27.5 kilometres (17 miles) long by 11 kilometres (9 miles) wide, Gozo is 14.5 kilometres (9 miles) long by 8 kilometres (5 miles) wide, while Comino is only about 2.5 square kilometres (1 square mile) large. There are also the uninhabited rock outcrops of Cominotto, Filfla, and Selmunett.

No nation has seen and endured, in the march of time, similar signal events and yet managed to preserve such a singular national identity. Occupied and controlled in turn by the most powerful maritime nation of the time, Malta has absorbed in its culture, foreign traits, customs, and idiom without sacrificing its purely Maltese identity, leading to the evolution, rather than the overwhelming, of the Maltese nation. Through perseverance and sheer doggedness, the Maltese evolved their character as an array of occupying powers held sway over them: the Phoenicians and the Carthaginians (800-218 BC), the Romans and the Byzantines (218 BC-AD 870), the Arabs (870-1091), the Normans, the Swabians, and the Angevins (1091-1282), the Spanish (1282-1530) the Order of St John of Jerusalem (1530-1798), the French (1798-1800), and, lastly, with the consent of the Maltese, the British (1800-1964). In 1964 Malta gained its independence. And yet, through this period of almost 3,000 years, the Maltese character remained unscathed.

Similarities between the Great Siege of 1565 and that of the Fascist forces in World War II cannot but impress the student

Map of the Maltese Islands – Early XVI Century

of world history. Both battles, 400 years apart, were fought for one and the same purpose, the destruction of the one obstacle in the invader's quest for domination over the Mediterranean and thus the conquest of the lands that surround the 'middle sea'.

It is so uplifting to take note and to enjoy the innumerable printed works that, since the 1960s, have provided serious studies about the island, its people, their struggles in peace and in war, and their triumph with the independence they finally gained.

It is to these works and to the earlier historians who fascinated me in my younger days, that I am so indebted for improving my

The Great Siege Monument, in Valletta

poor knowledge of the history of my native land. Since my retirement I have poured over these superbly-written works [see Bibliography] and reviewed and revised my original writings over again and over again. The result, I hope, will prove to be of some little value to student and layman alike, as, according to reports received, the broadcasts of this manuscript have originally done to the listeners of the Maltese hour on 4EB radio station in Australia.

There is one more important point which is very important to me and, I hope, to all other traditionalists. The folklore of a nation is an integral part of its traditional and documented history. It carries within it the beliefs of the people and through the people it flows from one generation to the other. If it is discarded, one day that country will have no living history. It should be kept alive, recorded, documented, sung, and recited; in this way the events of one's forefathers will live for ever in word and memory. That is why I have included so much folkloristic tradition relevant to this period in the history of my mother-country.

Charles Mula

Introduction

In 1978 six men, of whom I had the privilege to be one, got together to set up an ethnic radio station in Brisbane, Australia. The authorities of the time were refusing the pleas of the local ethnic communities to establish one, the excuse being that they were only 'small individual communities', to which should be added the fact they had no big electoral clout. Yet we eventually succeeded in realizing our dream with the help of some well-wishers. Soon the multi-lingual radio was on air as Radio 4EB.

As the co-ordinator for the Maltese hour, it was my responsibility to build up and present, together with other broadcasters, my wife Julia, Mrs Blanche Mifsud and her daughter, Mrs Josette Lloyd, and Mr Manuel Mercieca, a programme schedule for Maltese listeners in our native tongue. Soon it started to become clear to us that we were not sharing with our children, especially those born in Australia, the ancient and rich culture of our native land. These children were being brought up in an Australian (Anglo-Saxon) atmosphere and were more at home conversing in English than their parents' language, which language, together with other ethnic ones, was being, deliberately or not, suppressed by successive Australian governments by stressing the need for total assimilation through the educational institutions. Consequently, these children had very little, if any, knowledge of the land and culture of their parents.

To counteract such attitude, I thought of starting a series of talks on the history of Malta. Here was a chance, through the medium of the radio, to reach a large number of Maltese children who would listen to and become enraptured by stories of chivalry and bravery on the battlefield and of the glorious history of their fathers' native land. In addition, non-Maltese listeners would be able to share with us and enjoy some of the culture and history of the tiny Maltese nation, thus adding our culture to the cauldron of the different cultures that will one day form post-war multi-cultural Australia.

It was, therefore, decided to present these talks in English in order to reach as many people as possible, Maltese or otherwise.

My thoughts flew to my school days when our history master, Mr Paul Farrugia, managed to keep the enthusiasm of his students on the boil by his unique method of teaching history, which, in the 1930s, usually meant the memorizing of a series of names of kings and dates of 'significant' events. Mr Farrugia's method, however, was to sit on a student's desk with his feet resting on the chair, and, in such an unmasterly position, enter into a series of discussions on the period of history in question. To this gentleman and scholar, I owe all the love for history enkindled in me ever since.

Until the 1930s, Maltese history was not given much importance in Maltese schools. During this period which witnessed dramatic changes in the political life of the island, Albert V. Laferla's *The Story of Man in Malta* was published in serial form. This publication opened up for me a cavern full of wondrous treasures, while the late Mr Farrugia lit the torch and led me deeper and deeper into this maze of historical wonderment. I went further in my research and looked up other works on medieval Malta and on the occupation of the island by the Order of St John of Jerusalem.

And so it came about, many decades later, that I found myself writing episodes on Maltese history. The period I chose was naturally that most wonderful and fascinating period of valour and human endeavour in our art and culture. It was the period when princes ruled the island with splendour and service to humankind. These years were as illustrious for the island as those it would experience, four centuries later, during World War II and by the gaining of independence in 1964. This latter memorable event I did not, unfortunately, have the privilege to participate in.

Mrs Josette Lloyd Mifsud kindly agreed to read over the air, week after week, this series of talks. Her job was not easy since my manuscripts were the most illegible scribbles one could ever attempt to read, and when these scripts were presented minutes before the broadcast, one could see beads of perspiration coming down her face in front of the microphone. Thanks to her and to her mother, Mrs Blanche Mifsud, to Mr Manuel Mercieca, and to my wife Julia, who supported me throughout, this programme first went on air in March 1979. And that is how these writings came to be.

Charles Mula

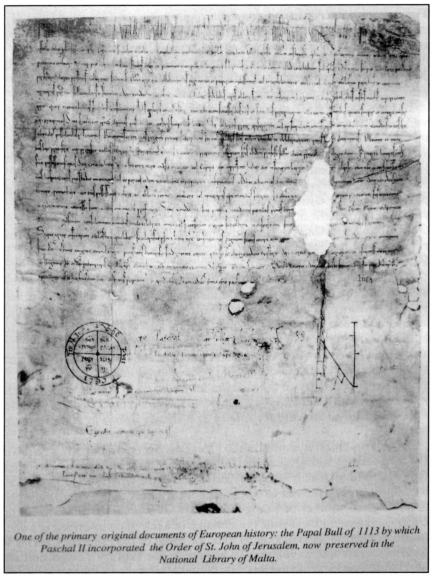

One of the primary original documents of European history: the Papal Bull of 1113 by which Paschal II incorporated the Order of St. John of Jerusalem, now preserved in the National Library of Malta.

Pope Paschall II's Bull of 1113,
granting ecclesiastical recognition to the Order

The Origin of the Knights Hospitallers

Samuel Rogers wrote thus of the knights of St John of Jerusalem:

'That chosen band; valiant, invincible
So long renowned as Champions of the Cross
In Rhodes, in Malta.'

It was in Malta that the Order of St John came to be called 'Illustrious' and 'The bulwark of Christendom'. Most of the noble houses of Europe vied with each other for the favour of having their sons accepted in the brotherhood which imposed strict rules and obligations upon the aspirants. It was, therefore, all the more imperative for the reigning houses of Europe to have their national langue seen as the best and the richest, well stocked with the most noble and most valiant of their subjects. They vied with each other for battle honours, encouraging brave deeds on the battlefield, while living in grandeur and opulence in their quarters which were known as auberges.

In a glass case in the National Library of Malta at Valletta there is displayed one of the primary original documents of European history. On this tattered parchment, the Charter of Incorporation, dated 1113, Pope Paschal II granted to 'His venerable son Gerard, founder and provost of the Hospital in Jerusalem', the ecclesiastical recognition of 'The Order of the Hospital of St John of Jerusalem'. By this means the new brotherhood was taken under the direct protection of the Holy

See. Of special interest is the fact that one of the signatories of this document was, as if by prophecy, John, bishop of Malta.

The venerable Gerard and the foundation of the Order of St John of Jerusalem

As soon as the Christian Church emerged from persecution, Christian pilgrims from the western world started to travel by overland routes to the holy places in Jerusalem, the land sanctified by the life, death, and resurrection of Jesus Christ. The journey was hard and beset with danger of attacks by thieves, Persians, and Arabs of Muslim faith. Diseases such as pestilence, dysentery, and malaria was yet another scourge. Before Byzantine Jerusalem fell into Muslim hands, the pilgrims that survived the journey went assured of a friendly welcome to the holy places; but after the capture of Syria and Palestine and, a few years later, Egypt by the Arabs, the welcome the Christian pilgrims received, depended on the sentiments of the individual Muslim ruler of the time. Some were tolerant and friendly, others not so friendly, while others were tyrannical. One of the early Arab rulers who had friendly and happy relations with Christians allowed the building of a hospice for the accommodation of pilgrims, the first of a series of such establishments in the Holy Land. By the time of Pope Gregory the Great (603) there was a hospice to care for the sick and tired pilgrims and all those others who were wounded or injured on the overland route.

In 1009 the Fatimate, Khalif Hatrim, a fanatical and demented tyrant, lord of the Saracen world, razed the Holy Sepulchre to the ground and it lay waste for 30 years. All Christian property established by Charlemagne in the Holy Land was seized and it was not until after Hakim's death in 1021 that greater safety in travel revived pilgrimages to the Holy Land. However, with later Muslim princes, especially those of the Seljuk dynasty, persecuting pilgrims, the desire of Western Christendom to regain possession of the Holy Land grew as complaint after complaint of the ill-treatment of pilgrims reached the west. This was the period when the crusades tried to wrest the Holy Land from the hands of the 'Infidel'. The western world started to believe in the establishing of a safer sea route to the Holy Land which would also increase maritime commerce with the eastern shores of the Mediterranean. Merchants from Amalfi, Venice, and Pisa vied with each other for supremacy in trade with the Levant.

Towards the end of the century, following the call of Pope Urban II for a 'Crusade in defence of the Cross', people started to offer themselves to fight the enemies of the Christian Church and to liberate the Holy Places. Peter the Hermit's crusade was a disaster. However, in what is recognized as the First Crusade, organized by the pope under the leadership of Godfrey de Bouillon, Jerusalem was captured in July 1099.

The Benedictine Order had established an abbey dedicated to St Mary of the Latins from moneys mostly contributed by the merchants of Amalfi. It is believed by some that these Benedictines also came from the same region. In conjunction with their monastic duties, these monks also looked after a hospice within the abbey grounds. By 1080 they had established a regular hospice service in a house on the site where the angel was believed to have announced to Zacharias that his wife, Anna, would conceive a son (St John the Baptist) in her old age. For this reason the hospice was dedicated to St John the Baptist. As a result of the expansion of this humanitarian service, the monks had to relinquish the tending of the sick to non-professed laymen who, adopting the Augustinian Rule, had volunteered to take over this work of charity yet keeping their confraternity completely separate from the monastic order.

By 1113, this brotherhood, under the direction of an Amalfitan

merchant named Gerard, later to be known as the Blessed
Gerard, grew so much that Pope Paschal II gave it
ecclesiastical recognition by a papal bull, *Pie Postulatio
Voluntatis*, under the title of 'The Hospital of St John the
Baptist'. Thus they became known as the Hospitallers of St
John the Baptist.

As it expanded, this brotherhood built daughter-houses in
various cities in Italy and along the high ways and ports leading
to the Holy Land. It also paved the way for other similar religious
organizations, soon to recognized as chivalric orders, to be
formed, notably the knights Templar founded in 1120 and who
followed the Cistercian Rule and the Teutonic Order founded
in 1198 during Pope Innocent's pontificate.

Lords and merchants who were made welcome in these houses,
looked after, and healed of their wounds, showed their gratitude
by bestowing on the Order portions of their estates; others chose
to join this brotherhood and devote their lives to the care of the
pilgrims. After Gerard's death in 1130, his successor, Raymond
du Puy, carried out a recruitment drive in Europe and moved
his quarters to new buildings nearer to the church of the Holy
Sepulchre.

So it came about that the Order grew in wealth and power with
so many aristocratic young men fighting with the Cross against
the Crescent. Its original responsibilities of tending the sick
and the poor were later extended to waging a perpetual war
against Islam in the eastern Mediterranean. Their influence
grew as the war against the Muslim world went on for centuries,
while the Order became a most formidable military instrument
of the Christian States whose rulers sometimes found the
Hospitallers to be as unruly in peace as they were valiant in
war.

The Order's newly-acquired influence and possessions gave it a quasi-independent militant status. Raymond de Puy, successor to the Blessed Gerard, acknowledged this militancy by officially renaming it 'The Military Order of Knights Hospitallers of St John the Baptist of Jerusalem', taking the title of grand master, and dividing the Order into three classes of service: knights, chaplains, and serving brothers. The grand master administered the Order with the help of a chapter general.

Battles against Muslim forces were won and lost and the Christian powers were forced to retreat from the Holy Land. The last stronghold was Acre from where they were finally driven by Saladin who destroyed the main forces of the Hospitallers and the Templars at the battle of Hattim.

Following the fall of Acre, the small remnant of the Templars and the Hospitallers settled in Cyprus in 1191. King Richard I of England, who captured Cyprus on his way to the Holy Land, sold the island to Godfrey de Guy of Lusignan, former king of Jerusalem, who was succeeded by his brother, Aimery.

King Aimery, who also became king-consort of the kingdom of Jerusalem through marriage to Queen Isabella, heiress to the throne of Jerusalem, was not, however, keen about them at all and wanted to get rid of them and their quarrels as soon as possible. He was, therefore, greatly relieved when the knights of St John under Grand Master Foulques de Villaret invaded Rhodes in 1306; and by 1310, the whole island was under their control, making Villaret the virtual monarch of an island nation. Consequently Villaret considered himself as the 'sovereign of the island'. This presumption was greatly encouraged by Pope Clement V.

The island kingdom was then in a state of decay. Villaret did his utmost to settle his knights in such a beautiful and bountiful surroundings and immediately started on a campaign to clear the Turks out of the island. In 1309 Clement V confirmed the

Grand Master Foulques de Villaret

Hospitallers' occupation and sovereignty of Rhodes, which they were to rule as sovereign rulers for 200 years. During this period, with no hope of recapturing the Holy Land (the original purpose of the establishment of the Order), the knights built a fleet of fighting ships, mastered the art of sea-warfare, and became the scourge of Muslim shipping. The Turks decided that this hornet's nest had to be wiped out. In 1480, during the grandmastership of Pierre d'Aubusson, Mehmet II attacked the island with a large armada. The knights, however, successfully held out for many months. In 1522 Suleiman the Magnificent again laid siege to Rhodes. Several attacks were made both from the sea and from land. After five months of bitter fighting and having run out of munitions, Grand Master Philippe Villiers L'Isle Adam succumbed to the pleas of the Rhodiots and the urging of his council to give up the fight, reluctantly accepted Suleiman's offer to 'surrender with all dignity and with all battle honours'. It is said that Suleiman wept to see such valiant men marching out and embarking, so steadfast and so proud.

On 1 January 1523, L'Isle Adam and the surviving knights embarked on three ships and sailed out of Rhodes to Civitavecchia by way of Candia (Crete) and Messina, where they sojourned for four years seeking for a place to settle. Venice could not help lest they jeopardized their trade with the Turkish empire, which now extended deep into Eastern Europe and along North African shores. The only dark spot in the Muslim world was Spain, where the *Riconquista* had begun in the fifteenth century, and which, in the sixteenth century, was extending its power in North Africa where they captured Tripoli in 1510. Spain was now arguably the leading naval power in the Mediterranean and the main defender of Christendom.

As for the Order of St John, this was the last element of the three great military Orders that had been born out of the Crusades. The most powerful Order, that of the Knights

Templar, had been suppressed early in the fourteenth century accused of idolatry and other heinous crimes. The second, the Teutonic Order, never recovered from its defeat at Tanenburg.

The Order soon evolved its characteristic form, grouping its members on the basis of nationality under eight langues which reflected the political realities of the time: Auvergne, Provence, France, Aragon, Castille, Italy, Germany, and England. To each of these, in Rhodes as well as later in Malta, was entrusted the defence of one sector of the fortifications. It was, in a sense, a league of Christian nations banding together against Islam.

The Order was also divided into five groups with definite duties, but all, whether fighting man or priest, were united by the triple vows of poverty, chastity, and obedience. First came the military group, the knights of justice, who in time came to dominate over the other four groups. An aspirant to this group had to be of pure aristocratic blood and untainted honour. The second in line were the conventual chaplains. They were the workers of the Church and the hospitals. All clergymen were eligible to the position of bishop of the Order or prior. The third arm consisted of the serving brothers or sergeants whose service was wholly of a military nature. The fourth and fifth divisions were honorary knights nominated by the grand master, known magistral knights and knights of grace respectively.

The Order was governed by four different councils, each with a separate function: the complete, the ordinary, the secret, and the criminal councils. Powers of government were vested in a council presided over by the grand master or his lieutenant. This council was either 'ordinary' or 'complete' and included the head of each langue (known as 'pilier') and all the knights grand cross residing in the Convent who were called 'conventual bailiffs'.

The Order chose the eight-pointed cross as its emblem, the eight points traditionally held to represent the eight beatitudes and the four arms the four virtues of prudence, temperance, fortitude, and justice.

The pilier of each langue on his appointment was officially given a post in the administration of this Order, as follows:

Provence   Grand Preceptor in charge of the treasury
Auvergne   Grand Marshal in charge of all matters military
France   Grand Hospitaller in charge of the Infirmary
Italy   Admiral in charge of the fleet
Aragon   Grand Conservator in charge of supply and distribution
England   Grand Turcopolier in charge of the cavalry and the coastguard
Germany   Grand Bailiff in charge of the fortified outposts
Castille   Grand Chancellor in charge of the chancery.

Meanwhile, not one of the sovereign houses of Europe offered a home to the Order; no one wanted them as they had grown

The Act of Donation ceding the Maltese Islands to the Knights Hospitallers
(National Library of Malta, Valletta)

arrogant and too powerful and independent. How then did the
Order of St John come to settle in Malta? How did this insigni-
ficant little island capture the admiration of friend and foe
alike and earn such immortal admiration in the annals of world
history?

It was Charles V of Spain who came to the Order's rescue,
primarily to spite his arch-enemy, King Francis I of France.
Charles chose a tiny speck of his vast empire on which to put
this band of upstarts out of harm's way, and as far away from
him as possible. A document, in the National Library of Malta,
bears the haughty signature of Charles and his queen, Joanna
the Mad. It says, *'I, the King, bestow the islands of Malta, Gozo,
and Comino on the knights of St John in order that they perform
in peace the duties of their Religion for the benefit of the Christian
Community and to employ their forces and arms against the
perfidious enemies of the Holy Faith.'* The annual 'fee' was the
presentation of a falcon to the viceroy of Sicily, then a
dependency of Spain, on All Saints' Day.

The Knights of St John in Malta

The knights hospitallers of the military Order of St John of Jerusalem, later to be better known as the 'knights of Malta', grew from a kindly and humane Order of Hospitallers attending to the sick and the pilgrims in the Holy Land into a very powerful and haughty sovereign Order in which the noble houses of Europe vied to have its scions accepted. However, when Charles V granted them Malta 'that they may perform the duties of their Religion in peace and employ their forces against the enemy of the Holy Faith', the islanders were furious. In 1428, King Alfonso of Aragon had reconfirmed them their ancient privileges after they had redeemed their island for a substantial cash payment of 30,000 gold florins, the sum for which the monarch used to pawn Malta to one feudal lord after another. This sum was collected from all Maltese man and woman, high or low, rich or poor, who freely gave all their gold to redeem their land from the avaricious feudal lords.

On the payment of these 30,000 gold florins, Alfonso had sworn on the four gospels that Malta would never be transferred to any other sovereignty. When the island was offered to the knights, the Maltese nobles, such as the Murina Gattos, the Inguanezes, the Stagnos, and the Navas (and some of these families who had originated from, or had inter-married with, the ancient Siculo-Aragonese aristocracy still survive as the most ancient nobility of Malta) were indignant that they were being traded about in such a callous and faithless manner. The clergy also were very apprehensive of the new rulers as the

Pope Clement VII and Emperor Charles V

newcomers were under the immediate protection of the Holy
See and they feared that the ecclesiastical rule of the bishop of
the island would be subjected to the grand masters of the
Religion. The Church, the nobility, and the people were
indignant that, after having redeemed their island, they were
again being ceded to other foreign rulers who, as later years
showed, were to take away their parliament (*Università*) and
their free institutions and interfere with the sacred privileges
of their bishops. This institution was later to snub the local
aristocracy further by refusing membership to their sons whose
noble lineage and titles antedated the Order's occupation of
Rhodes. Whilst the Maltese were furious with Charles V for
breaking Alfonso's oath and selling off the island for a mere
falcon, the Order was just as unhappy and quite reluctant to
take up the offer.

The Order, being loaded with the liability of the fortress of Tripoli together with Malta, were anything but enthusiasm. Grand Master L'Isle Adam sent a commission which, to make matters worse, gave a very unfavourable account of the island and its people. They described the island as a mere barren rock without vegetation, with scanty soil and very little water. The island's main centre of habitation consisted only of an old deserted town which served as its capital. The commissioners did not even mention the town's official name, Città Notabile, which had been bestowed upon it by Alfonso V. Città Notabile would undergo a further name-change to Città Vecchia following the building of the new city of Valletta. The commissioners also mentioned two other small towns nestling in the shelter of a natural and well-protected harbour, namely Birgu and Bormla which were a warren of narrow twisting little streets and lanes and not more than fishing hamlets. Scattered around the barren island, the commissioners continued, were a number of hamlets. The population they calculated to be around 12,000, speaking a sort of Moorish tongue, eking out a miserable existence from their bare lands and exposed to periodical raids by Barbary corsairs. There were no amenities, the commissioners lamented, scarcely any resources, and certainly many perils. So discouraging was the report that there was talk of declining Charles' offer. Only the harbours and creeks with their safe anchorages induced the knights to resign themselves with any sort of grace to the new venture. They grimly contrasted their occupation of a barren place to the pleasant hillsides and smiling valleys of Rhodes, where they had enjoyed their lovely city by the sea, set in luxurious vegetation.

The knights, despite their protests, actually sailed to their new home on 26 October 1530. There they were to rule for more than two-and-a-half centuries, until, on 12 June 1798, the French fleet, under the command of Napoleon Bonaparte, entered the Grand Harbour and took possession of the island without much of a fight. And so the rule of the Order of St John ended in ignominy when Grand Master Hompesch and some of his old followers left Malta, having surrendered the island without a decent struggle. For the first time, the boast that the battle standard of the Order had never been lowered to any foe was ignominiously shattered. Thus the islands fell into the hands of a foreign power, and the Maltese would again have to struggle to free themselves from foreign oppression to regain their liberty.

Phillipe Villiers de L'Isle Adam

1530-34

Because of the commission's unfavourable account, the council had almost declined Charles's offer. However, the splendid harbours and creeks that offered such safe anchorage for their fleet, proved decisive and they decided to give it a try. So the knights of the Order of St John, also known as 'the Religion', sailed from Sicily and set foot on Maltese soil on 26 October 1530.

The knights brought with them the great carrack of Rhodes, the *Sant'Anna*. From this famous flagship, the musicians' gallery (with its six exquisite panels depicting the story of Adam and Eve) in the throne room of the grand master's palace at Valletta is believed to have come. The knights also brought a relic of their patron saint, the right hand of St John the Baptist, the silver processional cross (still to be seen in the cathedral at Mdina), and other rich ecclesiastical treasures and vestments. Their generous victors at Rhodes also allowed them to take with them their unique and precious archives, still happily preserved in the National Library of Malta. They also gave permission

Phillipe Villiers de L'Isle Adam

The great carrack

Our Lady of Philermos

for those Greek citizens of Rhodes, who wished to accompany them, to do so. These refugees established, first in Birgu and then in Valletta, the Greek Uniate Church. This church in Valletta, which as a student at the Lyceum in the 1930s I liked to visit, was unfortunately destroyed in the Second World War but has since been rebuilt.

In 1530 Valletta did not exist. Instead there was a bare and uninhabited ridge of rock known as Xeb-er-ras, meaning 'the light off the point' or 'head', because of the existence of a tower, built in the fifteenth century by the Aragonese which served as a lighthouse to guide shipping in and out of both harbours and to guard against Turkish attacks.

A picture, by the French artist Antoine Favray, hanging in the palace, Valletta, portrays the pageantry of L'Isle Adam receiving the keys of Mdina which the commission had described as an old deserted town, standing on high ground in the middle of the island and which today, floodlit at night, looks like a fairy castle floating on air. Favray's picture portrays L'Isle Adam walking in ceremonial procession under a *baldakkin* held aloft by six priors of the Order. Preceding the *baldakkin* there is the ceremonial cross of the Religion, flanked by two pages, one bearing the grand master's battle sword and the other Charles V's charter. Behind the *baldakkin*, the various langues are depicted in procession in strict order of priority, unarmed and in ceremonial dress.

Some historians record that the first meeting had to be abandoned because the knights of the various langues marched in their impressive armour which was deemed offensive for such an occasion. The *Università*, made up of the nobility and the jurats or magistrates, refused to come out of the gate of the walled city to receive the delegation and hand over the keys of the city to an armed contingent, as that, they believed, would indicate a surrender.

Antoine Favray: Grand Master L'Isle Adam taking possession of Mdina

'We are not a conquered people,' the jurats said, 'and, although we are prepared to hand over the keys of sovereignty to the Order, this is being done of our free will and subject to the Order proclaiming that the grand master will defend and uphold the freedom of the people and guarantee the privileges of the *Università*.' They also insisted that they would not come out until the grand master declared that he and all subsequent grand masters, after their election, would swear that they would walk to the gate of Mdina to receive the silver keys of the city from the *capitano della verga* (captain of the rod) and the four jurats, and also swear to them that he would maintain the rights and privileges of the *Università*. L'Isle Adam had to accept this demand if he were to establish a home for his Order in true pomp and grandeur befitting the representatives of the select nobility of Europe, from which the several langues drew their members.

L'Isle Adam walked in procession, the only armour allowed being his own sword which was carried by his page, and was met at the gates by the captain of the rod or, as he was known in Maltese, the *Hakem*. After taking the oath as demanded, L'Isle Adam was handed the keys of the city, which signified the handling over of authority; only then was he allowed to march to the cathedral where the bishop of Malta intoned the *Te Deum*.

In Mdina L'Isle Adam visited the residence of the De Nava family who were the castellans of the *castello a mare* or Fort St Angelo. He also established the first conventual chapel of the Order in the church of St Lawrence at Birgu where he installed the priceless icon of Our Lady of Philermos. This icon was one of the few precious items miraculously saved from the fire that destroyed this church in 1532 and which was replaced with a basilica which was to serve as the Order's conventual church until its transfer to St John's in Valletta in 1571.

The langues immediately set themselves outbidding each other to find the most comfortable lodgings for their own members, who from the beginning showed signs of restlessness resulting in regularly quarrelling with each other. They were still hoping that the 200,000 *scudi* given to L'Isle Adam by Henry VIII of England would go a long way to win back their much beloved Rhodes.

In one of the narrow streets of Birgu, Majjistral Street (North-West Street), the auberge of England still stands; it has been restored and functions as a public library. Next door to it is the residence of Sir Oliver Starkey, the famous lieutenant and confidant of grand master Valette and one of the last remaining three knights of the langue of England. It was Valette who built this auberge in 1559 after Queen Mary restored to the Order the latter's property in England, only for Queen Elizabeth to re-confiscate them. In Birgu there are also the original auberges of Italy, of Germany, and of France, Auvergne, and Provence combined, the most ample of them all.

The grand master also chose to settle in Birgu, taking residence in the *castel a mare*, as he considered it necessary to live amongst his knights in order to keep discipline. He immediately started to take measures to fulfil the Order's primary function of hospitallers. By 1533 the new hospital was in operation looking after the sick and the destitute. For security at nightfall he provided a prison for slaves engaged in the service of the Order. He also did not neglect his favourite pastime, hunting. On the promontory of L-Isla, then also known as St Julian's hill presumably because of a small chapel dedicated to the saint, L'Isle Adam built a large house, which became known as the Magistral House, where he and his guests could rest after hunting in the orchards he planted.

However, at that time a new menace was making itself felt in the Mediterranean: the terrible and mighty Barbarossa

was sweeping the seas with eight galleys. The sovereigns of
Europe, fearing for the fate of the knights as the latter were
right in the way of this scourge of the seas, suggested to
L'Isle Adam that he transfer himself and his men to a safer
country, such as Sicily. To this the grand master replied, 'I
have never run away from a fight in front of the enemies of
Religion and they know that very well. Am I to give such a
bad example to my brothers to preserve the remaining years
of my waning life?'

L'Isle Adam focused all his attention to the building of
fortifications around Birgu and Bormla and at L-Isla where
Fort St Michael was built. He reinforced the fortifications of
Fort St Angelo, creating a formidable defence in the inner part
of the harbour. He also rebuilt the chapel of St Anne in Fort St
Angelo in addition to the one dedicated to the Virgin Mary.
Moreover, he saw to the strengthening of the walls of Mdina.
There remained the problem of the open and poorly-defended
high cliffs on the north shore of the harbour where there was a
small watch tower and a chapel dedicated to St Elmo, patron
saint of seamen, and which later, after an enemy raid, the
viceroy of Sicily had fortified by a wall. These high cliffs on the
north shore of the harbour presented great dangers to the
southern shores as they overlooked Fort St Angelo. Plans were
also prepared to defend this highland of Xeb-er-ras.

Beset by internal troubles within the Order, and depressed by
the poverty of the land, the 72-year-old grand master retired to
the church of the Franciscan Minors outside Mdina where he
died on 21 August 1534, almost four years after setting foot on
the island. In Malta he had courageously begun a programme
of construction. The loss of finance from property as a result of
the Reformation in England, Germany, Sweden, and Denmark,
did much to hamper his work and break his heart. His heart
was buried in the Franciscan church where he had died. His
embalmed body was laid in state in the chapel of Our Lady in

Fort St Angelo

S. Anne Chapel at St Angelo

Fort St Angelo for several days where the inhabitants went to pay their homage and respect, filing past him and kissing his hands.

Monument of Grand Master de l'Isle Adam

(St John's Church, Valletta)

The inscription on his mausoleum in Fort St Angelo reads:

'Brother Phillipe Villiers de L'Isle Adam, Master of the Hospital, after having lifted his Order from the fall into which it had precipitated, and given it back a peace which was sought for ten years, established himself in Malta, where he dedicated by invocation of Jesus, this little chapel destined to be his burial place. He died at the age of over seventy years on 22 August in the year of Our Lord 1534'.

His remains were later transferred to the crypt of the grand masters in the conventual church of St John's, Valletta.

Piero del Ponte

1534-35

The new grand master, Piero del Ponte, hailed from Piedmont, and was a descendant of the ancient family of Casal-Gros and Lombriax. He was governor of the island of Lango when Rhodes fell to the Turks. He was still there when he received the news of his election as the forty-fourth grand master of the Order and the second in Malta.

By this time the terror of the seas, the marauding Barbarossa, was sweeping the Mediterranean and harassing lands around Malta. He captured Tunis and had cast his eyes on Tripoli, then under Spain, and was also chasing Christian shipping.

Del Ponte sent powerful help to Tripoli and informed Charles V of the imminent danger that Tripoli could be lost. The emperor responded by sending an army to Tunis to try and retain this stronghold on the shores of North Africa.

The Order was also interested in defeating Barbarossa for many

Grand Master Piero del Ponte

other reasons, especially to deny him a vantage port from where he could raid Maltese shores, plunder villages, and carry Maltese people away to slavery. So 18 brigantines were dispatched to Sardinia where Charles V was rallying his armada to sail to North Africa. Taking the enemy by surprise to the shouts of the battle cry 'St John', they were victorious and marched on Tunis.

The enraged Barbarossa ordered that 20,000 Christians, including many Maltese, were to be massacred. Luckily, news of the Spanish forces closing in on the city and of the fate that awaited them got round to the imprisoned prisoners. The following day, the slaves rose in revolt and the large mob of them, led by an Italian knight, took to arms in the streets of Tunis. So fierce was the fighting that the garrison and the inhabitants, taken by surprise, were obliged to flee to escape the onslaught. Barbarossa himself had to follow suit to save his life.

But, according to tradition, the master of a pirate ship, which had earlier been taken to Tunis, one called Paolo Samuel, succeeded in overpowering the guards and set himself and all prisoners free. Samuel, his crew, and a number of Maltese slaves headed to the port where their ship lay at anchor. As the fleeing slaves stormed the ship, praying that the secret of a valuable cargo pillaged from Rhodes, was still intact. To the battle cry of 'Santa Maria', they seized their old ship and immediately set sail for Malta. According to the same tradition, one of their first acts on board ship, was to retrieve their secret and sacred cargo which consisted of a small statue of Our Lady, which had been stolen from an old Christian church in Rhodes. The liberated slaves immediately placed the small statue on the prow of the vessel as they were sure it would miraculously guide them safely to Malta. By the following morning the ship lay at anchor under the shadow of the walls of Fort St Michael. On that fine morning the captain and his men marched in procession, carrying the little statue aloft towards L-Isla and deposited the precious cargo in the chapel of St Julian. This tradition also has it that the same statue played another glorious part in the momentous history of the island and of L-Isla. The little statue of Our Lady came to be called as *il-Bambina* ('the little baby girl', in honour of the birth of the Virgin Mary) while its feast was later to become known as *Il-Vitorja* (Our Lady of Victories).

Back in Tunis, the revolt of the slaves had come as such a surprise that the garrison thought that the Christian forces had broken into the city. The Muslim forces fled, leaving the city open to the invading forces and Spain regained its North African empire.

Del Ponte died on 18 November 1535, 15 months after his election. He had spent his time bringing some discipline into the Order. A simple and pious man, he was buried in the chapel of Our Lady of Victories (as it was later re-dedicated after 1565), in Fort St Angelo. Eventually his remains were interred in the crypt of St John's in Valletta.

Didiers de Saint Jaille

1535-36

After the death of del Ponte, the knights looked for a strong man to lead the faction-ridden Order. His successor, Didiers de Saint Jaille, was immediately hailed as one worthy of succeeding to the magistracy.

Soon after his arrival in Malta from Manosque, where he was bailiff, he landed into a great squabble between the langues of France and Italy, which together made up more than 80 per cent of the total knights on the island. These quarrels often led to fatal skirmishes in the streets.

The grand master soon found a way of diverting such energy away from the island and directing it against the enemy, the Turkish fleet, then ransacking the North African shores. With the fighting ships put to sea, the knights could spend their fury attacking Turkish ships and capturing valuable Muslim cargo and slaves.

Grand Master Didiers de Saint Jaille

Two views of the Crypt of the Grand Masters. Only two Grand Masters
are not burried in Malta, Didiers de Saint Jaille being one of them
(St John's Church, Valletta)

The knights fought a great battle to save their outpost of Tripoli. During this battle a cannonball hit the Turkish commander, killing him outright. As a result, the Turkish force fled and left the way open for the knights to march on Arcadia which they destroyed, taking a large number of prisoners.

The fleet of the Order then returned to Malta where they found their newly-elected grand master had died. During their absence, taking advantage of the ensuing peace at home, Saint Jaille had strengthened the battlements of St Angelo and dug a ditch to be able to cut off communication between the fort and Birgu as a precaution against a Turkish invasion. He died on 26 September 1536, just eleven months after his election. He is one of the two grand masters who ruled over Malta who is not buried in the island.

Juan d'Omedes

1536-53

Following the sudden and unexpected death of Saint Jaille, there was no lack of ambitious candidates from among all the valiant knights scattered throughout Europe.

The choice fell on a man from Aragon, who had served with distinction in the siege of Rhodes under L'Isle Adam and had lost an eye for his pains. His election ensured that the Order and Malta could again be considered to be under the protection of Charles V, bringing to an end the French hegemony over the Order. It took d'Omedes almost 18 months to assume his post. In fact, he arrived in Malta on 21 January 1538, and started on a long reign that lasted 17 years during which he went through peace and war and prepared the island for all emergencies. His charity and great love of the common man made him loved by all such men, while his sense of justice earned him the respect of all. His first shock after taking office came in 1540, when the property of the Order in England was confiscated by the English crown.

Grand Master Juan d'Omedes

In 1541 the outpost of Tripoli was in danger of falling to the enemy. D'Omedes, true Spaniard that he was, sent the might of the fleet of the Order and his most valiant captains to help save the city for Spain. The Turkish onslaught on the badly fortified and unprepared city was so great that the garrison asked for permission to abandon the city and many a commander left his post. It was left to the captain, Jean Valette, who, always sure of himself, regrouped his men, and defended the city. Tripoli was lost; even so the Turkish fleet left to take its revenge for the knights' stand by devastating Gozo.

Meanwhile in 1544, a civil war between the anti-Spanish French and Italian knights on the one hand, and the Spanish and the rest of the knights on the other, had broken out in Malta with dire consequences for the island and its people. Most knights opposed the election of d'Omedes; the French were upset for having lost their grip on the magistracy, and the Italians on the French side because they hated the idea of Spain's sovereignty. They accused d'Omedes of neglecting his magistral duties, spending most of his time at the Boschetto, enjoying himself watching animals feeding from the palace he had built away from the Magistral House on L-Isla point. According to the historian of the Order, Antonio Bosio, d'Omedes's avarice was responsible for the loss of Tripoli.

By 1546 the civil war had become so harsh that word got round to the enemy that the knights were destroying one another on the island and that Malta was wide open for assault. Such dangerous news reached the ears of the grand master.

D'Omedes had to use all his guile and good nature to restore order amongst the knights. The problem became even more complicated with the Maltese taking sides. The *Università* and the jurats (the nobility and the intelligentsia) supported the Spanish and Italian langues and ignored the grand master's plea for law and order. This offered them an opportunity to lash out at d'Omedes for failing to keep law and order and to bring justice to the poor working man. The merchants, on the other hand, were wholly behind the French knights. The French life was one of good living that had not been enjoyed since the days of L'Isle Adam; they hated the life of austerity and simple living d'Omedes advocated. They liked the work he created but not the encouragement to the labourer to earn and save and to better himself and his family life. This seemed to upset the order of things and the unwritten law of 'master and servant'.

The common man was all for his benefactor, d'Omedes, and would have been behind him to a man but they were still almost serfs, serving the nobility and the merchant gentry. They were torn and divided between their love and loyalty to their grand master hero on the one hand and their daily bread and butter on the other, and since an empty belly invariably wins the argument, each man followed his master. Thus d'Omedes was left to quieten the troubled waters on his own, which he partly succeeded in doing by posting the rebellious French knights, under the command of a French governor, out of the way in Tripoli.

In 1550 the corsair Dragut was appointed to the command of the Turkish navy in recognition of his ability to harass and capture Christian shipping. This gave him the opportunity of avenging his defeat at Mahdia and his humiliating capture on the island of Djerba. He swore he would go in and finish off the Order. A number of times he criss-crossed the channel between Malta and Gozo, but could not decide to march against the well-defended populated centres. It was easier to land in undefended Gozo or the northern shores of Malta, ravage the land, pillage the villages, and take slaves without opposition. The only shelter for the country people in the northern part of the island was Mdina, where they could hide behind the ramparts of the old city. At the sound of the cathedral bells announcing the landing of the Muslims, the villagers would grab a few personal belongings and what little food they had and hasten into Mdina. Those lucky to reach the walled city in time were safe, while the others, especially the young men, found themselves behind the oars of some Turkish galley. Women were raped and carried away to a lifetime of slavery and old men who offered resistance were slaughtered on the spot.

Gozo then had a small population. After each Muslim attack, those Gozitans who had escaped capture crossed to Malta. Some returned when the danger had passed while others settled on the larger island around Mellieħa and farther south and inland as Mosta, Mġarr, and Naxxar, so as to be nearer to Mdina and away from the constant Turkish raids. It is said that Dragut had a personal grievance against Malta and wanted to avenge his defeat by the knights at Mahdia. He is also said to nurtured a special grudge against Gozo where, during one of his raids, his younger brother, who was accompanying him, had been killed and his body carried away by the Gozitans. So Dragut, who had asked for the return of his brother's remains in vain, took revenge on Gozo and its people at every opportunity that arose.

In 1550 the fleet of the Order helped the Spanish to secure a foothold in North Africa at Susa, a small town on the coast of present-day Tunisia, the nearest point in Africa to Malta. This greatly irritated Suleiman the Magnificent who vowed that the knights must be destroyed once and for all. He immediately started to assemble a large armada of 110 galleys and a large number of smaller transport craft.

The news of these preparations reached d'Omedes but he refused to act, fully believing that these preparations were no threat to him and that there was no need to strengthen the defences of the island any more. He declared that he believed that this great Muslim armada was intended only to join the fleet of the king of France, then enjoying a temporary truce with the Muslims, against Spain, and would definitely not land in Malta.

The *Università* thought otherwise and sent word to Sicily for help. On the morning of 16 July, d'Omedes was hurriedly awakened to the news that the Turks were landing at Marsamxett where the fleet had anchored under the shadow of Mount Xeb-er-ras. The Turks, under Dragut, had this sheltered harbour all to themselves. No resistance was offered. D'Omedes, still incredulous, did nothing to stop the pillaging and burning of the villages as the corsairs marched towards the knights' stronghold of Fort St Angelo and Birgu. Before d'Omedes realized what was happening, the Turks were attacking Fort St Angelo.

The plea for help sent to Sicily by the *Università* got to the ears of a knight called Villegaignon who immediately took action and left in a small boat with a chosen crew of ten Maltese. They approached Malta under cover of darkness; landed just outside the harbour, and headed for Fort St Angelo to deliver a message from the king of Sicily. As they approached the beleaguered Fort St Angelo, they realized they were all too late; in fact d'Omedes and his knights were already preparing to surrender. Villegaignon had to break through but at the same time he saw his chance of playing a ruse on the enemy.

The plan was that two or three volunteers were to 'wander' behind enemy lines carrying a fake message from the king of Sicily. The volunteers, however, were not to make a move until the rest of the party got through into Fort St Angelo. Then, at the signal of a bonfire from the Fort, the volunteers would allow themselves to be caught. The plan worked very well. The bonfire was lit, and the volunteers strayed into the enemy lines at break of dawn. They were caught and taken to Dragut's tent. Under torture, they confessed that they were messengers of the king of Sicily and produced the fake message.

Dragut was shaken. The message said that the Venetian admiral, Doria himself, the only man that Dragut feared, was on his way with his fleet to rescue the besieged Order. This was enough for Dragut. The assault on Malta was only an adventure as his main aim was to capture Tripoli and finally clear the North African shores from the hold of Spain and the Crusaders. So as not to endanger his men and risk a defeat, he set sail and left Malta. Gozo, however, was not so lucky and Dragut ravished the island in keeping with his vow.

Some time later, news arrived of a fresh Turkish armada being assembled to annihilate Malta. This time the threat was taken seriously and the celebrated engineer Leone Strozzi, the prior of Capua, was recalled from banishment and to report to Malta to inspect the fortifications. He immediately pointed out the weaknesses of the defences around the harbour. He noticed the headland of Mount Xeberras set between the two harbours, the Grand Harbour and Marsamxett, and whose point therefore commanded the entrances to both harbours. Suggestions were made that new headquarters for the Order and a new city be built across the harbour from their actual base, on the south side of the harbour, on land on the north side that was not dominated by other higher ground, as was then the case with Fort St Angelo, Birgu, and Bormla. However, the treasury was impoverished and, although some plans were prepared, the idea was temporarily dropped.

Strozzi decided to build a fort on the strategic point. With no money in the treasury, it was the people of Malta, and those knights who had grown to love the island, who offered to donate the money and gifts for the building of the fortress. At the head of the peninsula, where there was already a watch tower and a chapel, a small star-shaped fort was erected under the direction of the Spanish engineer, Pietro Pardo, and named after St Elmo. This fort would, according to earlier plans, defend the two harbours on either side, the Grand Harbour and Marsamxett. However, the weakness of this fort was that it lay at the lowest part of the promontory and was dominated by higher terrain which provided a gun battery with a direct firing line into the fortress. Under the direction of the engineer Ferramolino, Fort St Angelo was also greatly strengthened: the moat was enlarged and deepened to guard it against land attack and a cavalier was also built to protect it from a sea attack. He also brought from Venice a huge chain that extended across Galley Creek from St Angelo to L-Isla, thus protecting the inner harbour. Pardo was also engaged to build a fort at L-Isla which was finished within a year and named St Michael.

Once these defences were completed, the grand master turned his attention to recapturing some of the African lands earlier lost to the Muslims. A successful attack on Zoara was undertaken but the post was lost again during the attack on Tripoli when the Order's attacking force was annihilated. This defeat had a terrible effect on the ageing grand master and hastened his death.

Also at this time, in 1553, news arrived that the queen of England was about to restore the Order's property in England. Unfortunately d'Omedes did not live to see the end of the negotiations for he died on 6 September 1553.

'His eyes were always open to keep peace in his Order and liberty for his subjects', so says the epitaph on d'Omedes's monument in the crypt of St John's. He died at the age of 80 years; his prudence and love of peace and docility nearly lost him and his Order the island of Malta and the respect of his subjects. In truth no one shed a tear for his demise.

Claude de la Sengle

1553-57

The Order now needed someone strong and determined to stand up to an enemy that was just as determined to annihilate the Knights as never before.

Claude de la Sengle seemed to be the man the Order was looking for. Born in France in 1494, he joined the Order at a very young age as a novice. His prudence and valour on the field of battle and his piety as a brother gained for him the highest dignities.

La Sengle was principally responsible for the success of the North African expeditions. He proved himself a clever diplomat by reconciling the viceroys of Sicily and Naples in their quarrel over the command of the expedition. As a result, he was appointed head of the langue of France and grand hospitaller. He also served as ambassador to Rome. On the death of d'Omedes, de la Sengle was elected the fifth grand master in Malta in December 1553.

Grand Master Claude de la Sengle

On his way to Malta, la Sengle was feted by the viceroy of Sicily and treated like a king. An able diplomat, he avoided getting involved and taking sides, and kept his mouth shut and promised nothing in spite of the many demands and favours being made on him. He could not offend either Spain or Sicily, especially as the latter supplied corn to Malta, and he could not afford to have this aid stopped.

During these festivities, the king of Spain sent his emissary to induce the new grand master to join the king's campaign to recapture Tunis. Rather than refuse outright, la Sengle replied that he could not reply before he submitted this request to the grand council of the Order. The ambassador followed him to Malta where the case was discussed actively. However, taking advantage of the rumours of a build-up of the Turkish fleet, the king's request had to be declined. Immediately the shipments of corn were stopped. Nevertheless the fleet of the Order continued to police the Mediterranean and to protect the very coasts that were refusing corn to the Maltese.

La Sengle carried on with determination and as more rumours of increased enemy activity were reaching the island, he reinforced all fortifications and enlarged Fort St Angelo. Fort St Michael was re-built while the *boschetto* (planted by L'Isle Adam) behind it was cleared for a new city to be built using the stone obtained from digging the ditches round the wall. He decreed that this city, built on the spit of land formerly known as L-Isla, should be called Senglea in his honour.

In 1555 a great disaster befell the island. A storm, the like of which had never been experienced before, broke over Malta on 23 September at dusk. The wild seas driven by a mighty northeast wind, the *grigal*, seemed to engulf all the land; huge trees were uprooted and vessels in port were flung onto land and smashed to pieces. Four galleys of the Order capsized and were lost. When calm returned, more than 600 corpses were seen floating in the sea. The population was in a state of shock. La Sengle went personally on foot visiting the disaster areas, consoling the bereaved families, and giving alms to those in need out of his own pocket.

With the threat of a new enemy attack, la Sengle built three galleys at his own expense to replace some of those lost in the storm. Philip II of Spain donated another two vessels and the grand prior of France another two. The pope sent valuable assistance and the corn shipments from Sicily were resumed. In short, the loss was so quickly replaced that Dragut was taken completely by surprise and completely routed when he attacked Gozo with a sizeable force. He had to leave behind a large number of Gozitan would-be slaves.

This year 1555 saw the beginning of the collection that was eventually to become the National Library of Malta. The grand master, in a general chapter, decreed that all the books of deceased knights were to be donated to the Order to establish a library for the use of conventual chaplains. This collection was augmented by other decrees by succeeding grand masters and donations from benefactors over the centuries.

La Sengle was by now completely exhausted. On 15 September 1557, he decided to retire to Mdina. He immediately retired to his bedchamber, tired after his long journey from Birgu. Next morning la Sengle was found dead in his bed. His heart was buried in the Carmelite church of the Annunciation outside Rabat. His body today lies in the crypt of St John's in Valletta.

La Sengle's memory lives in the fortified city which he founded and which bears his name, Senglea.

Jean Parisot Valette

1557-68

In 1515, a 20-year-old nobleman of the illustrious house of Quercy joined the Order as a brother knight in the langue of Provence. His name was Jean Valette known as Parisot. Described as a very handsome man, Valette was born in 1494 into an ancient and noble Proven al family of the house of the counts of Toulouse.

From childhood, he showed a single-minded attitude to life. He could speak French, Italian, Spanish, and Greek, as well as Arabic and Turkish, the latter two he learned as a galley slave. Having been schooled in the military arts, he was immediately despatched to overseas posts where he was engaged in many skirmishes with the enemy. It was in one of these engagements that he really began to appreciate the formidable enemy that he was destined to fight against in the years to come. He was captured in one such battle in Africa and made to serve on a galley where he was badly treated and swore that, when he became free, the Turks would pay for it dearly. This oath he

Grand Master Jean Parisot Valette

fulfilled in 1565 in the siege of Malta and, before that, in the sorties he led on North African shores. He was freed in a prisoner exchange.

After his release from captivity, Valette was appointed commander and sent to lead the defence of Tripoli. His military genius and valour earned him many promotions; he was appointed a bailiff grand cross, grand prior of St Giles, and lieutenant general of the failed expedition to Zoara. This expedition gave him a chance to demonstrate his leadership of his peers as well as of the common soldier. La Sengle, recognizing both the man and the wishes of the other knights, appointed Valette lieutenant grand master, thus nominating him as his successor.

Valette was elected grand master on 21 August 1557. His immediate thoughts turned to imposing the discipline he believed necessary if he was to defeat the Muslim enemy once and for all. Indisputably he was the greatest grand master of the Order which, under him, reached its highest glory.

As a first step he directed his energy in re-establishing harmony and discipline among the German and Venetian knights who had struck away on their own and had refused to pay their tributes to the Order for a long time. He also pardoned and released from prison the rebellious French knights D'Omedes had imprisoned. Valette also started on a project to reconquer Tripoli.

Valette's greatest wish was to hurt the Turks and humiliate his arch-enemy Suleiman called 'The Magnificent', ruler of the Ottoman empire. The Turks had fortified Tripoli as the best fortress in Africa. Tripoli was to the Turks what Malta was to the knights. In 1559 an expedition of 400 knights and 1,500 men left Malta for Messina to join the armada of his ally, the viceroy of Sicily. Things did not go at all well. The viceroy got himself embroiled in the capture of the island of Gelua, losing a large number of men. The remainder of the army was struck

Suleiman 'The Magnificent'

by an epidemic which decimated the attackers. As a result Valette decided to recall his men to Malta. Unfortunately for the viceroy, the retreating and weakened fleet was attacked by Turkish vessels and most of the ships and men were lost. The viceroy managed to escape leaving more than half his force behind. This defeat delivered a crippling blow to Spanish naval supremacy in the western Mediterranean.

Suleiman the Magnificent, the scourge of the Mediterranean and enemy of all things Christian, was by now an old man, but still ferociously determined that his rule and Islam should prevail over the Middle Sea and all lands bordering it.

Of all the forces barring his way, the most formidable and persistent were the knights of St John. Suleiman had only been 29 years of age when he had expelled the Order from Rhodes in 1522. He was 71 when he took his final oath to expel them from Malta and exterminate them forever, after which his forces would be free to roam all over the seas and ravage the lands far and wide in Europe and Africa. The recent victory over the Spanish fleet and the armies of the viceroy of Sicily bore testimony that nothing could stop him, once he had silenced that handful of knights in their island lair. Valette was now the grand master of those knights, the forty-eighth in line of succession and the sixth to reign in Malta.

Suleiman was losing his patience with the Order whose fleet continually harassed his vessels and his possessions. He therefore decided to take steps and stop the knights once and for all and to annihilate the 'bandits'. So he started to raise up a large armada to capture Malta and rid himself of the Order. Against Suleiman there was another old man of exactly the same age, Grand Master Valette, the arch-enemy of old.

When Valette got to know that Suleiman was building up large forces for a probable attack on Malta, he sought assistance from the viceroy of Sicily who sent corn and a small contingent of soldiers. Spain sent the newly-appointed captain general of the sea, Don Garcia de Toledo, in April 1565 to discuss the island's defence. He directed that the fort on the promontory of Xeberas, to which work Valette attended. Don Garcia also informed Valette that, on his return to Spain, he would ask Philip to prepare a large and well-equipped force to reinforce the garrison and in the meantime arrange for 1,000 men to be immediately sent from Sicily.

The grand master ordered all the knights abroad to come to Malta and in a few weeks the island was ready to meet the attack. Pope Pius IV sent men and materials and the king of Spain promised further help. The fortifications being ready, the four galleys of the Order that were in port were drawn up in the inner harbour and placed under constant guard. To make the inner harbour safer, a heavy chain boom brought from Venice was placed across the mouth of the deepest creek, Galley Creek, between St Angelo and L-Isla. This chain could be raised by means of a capstan to allow friendly ships through. Maltese fishermen, under the direction of an old and wily Maltese corsair named Burlò, made use of 1,000 slaves to secure the chain to a massive anchor embedded in the rock at one end and to a capstan at the other.

On the morning of 18 May 1565, the grand fleet of 180 ships of the Ottoman Empire in full sail appeared on the horizon. The warning gunfire from Forts St Elmo and St Angelo echoed all over the island. The alarm bells of Birgu and Mdina rang out to warn the Maltese living outside the walls of Birgu, Senglea, and Mdina who either fled to the protection of the fortifications or hid in caves, but not before destroying all the crops that could not be carried away, and poisoning all supplies of water.

If Valette had a single qualm about the outcome of this mighty thrust by his oldest enemy, it did not show in his bearing as he stood on the battlements of Fort St Angelo surveying the enemy fleet sailing towards Gallows Point, now known as Ricasoli Point.

The enemy fleet sailed past Point Xeberras but, to the amazement of the defenders, it did not try to land at Marsamxett. The armada kept on sailing south past Marsaxlokk Bay and passed between Wied iż-Żurrieq on the mainland and the islet of Filfla to anchor for the night under the cliffs of Mġarr. A scouting party sent ashore was engaged by cavalry from Mdina. This landing was only a ruse intended to make believe that the Turks intended to attack the north of the island before moving to the more fortified south. However, Valette, knowing fully whom he was dealing with, had sent that detachment of cavalry, led by great horsemen like de Nava and Indri Sahara, to follow the progress of the enemy fleet. By early dawn the fleet had changed course and was doubling back to lay anchor at Marsaxlokk Bay by late night of the following day. The force was reported to consist of 180 ships carrying an army of 8,000 special troops, the dreaded cavalry of Spahis and the famous Janizzary bowmen, personal guardians of the sultan, and backed by 38,000 foot soldiers under Pialì Pasha, the admiral of the fleet and son-in-law of Suleiman, and Mustapha Pasha, the army commander-in-chief and an old comrade and confidant of the sultan.

During the night of the twentieth the disembarkation of the invading army begun. A party was sent to reconnoitre the countryside for bases and water supplies. The wells at Marsa turned out to have been poisoned but the site was reported to be excellent for the main camp.

Preparations for the battle

The knights had been prepared for such a battle since their initiation into the Order. Through long years of training, they had gone through great suffering in battle practice in order to be accepted into the brotherhood. As page-boys or novices, they had to perform four 'caravans', that is six-month cruises of service on the galleys during which time they had to learn to navigate, handle the ship, stand to arms at all times, man the guns, and board enemy ships. Those who survived this long ordeal and showed valour and discipline gained their knighthood and could take their solemn vows of poverty, chastity, and obedience on reaching the age of 21. So, trained, armed, and inspired, the knights now prepared for Suleiman's assault. Under God and their master-leader, Valette, they were definitely *not* going to surrender.

Francesco Balbi, one of the soldiers in Fort St Michael, records in his account of the siege that the defenders consisted of 541 knights and sergeants-at-arms. Some three to four thousand Maltese regulars formed the main body of the defence. With the addition of the knights who had reached the island and some 400 Spanish soldiers from Sicily, Valette could muster in all a total force of eight to nine thousand men. Balbi states that the fighting force included the serving men and all classes of civilians, from professionals to manual workers, from farmers to tradesmen — in short anyone who could bear arms. Women and children helped wherever they could, while older folk attended to the duties of those called to arms.

Like a tower of strength, Valette toured the fortifications of Fort St Elmo to ensure that all was ready to withstand any attack by sea or land. Placing Bailiff Luigi Broglia in command and sending a few reinforcements under Colonel Mas, Valette blessed his brother-knights. Their orders were to stop any enemy ship trying to enter the Grand Harbour at any cost thus pre-empting any seaward attack on St Angelo and the inner harbour.

Even with such a formidable fortification as Fort St Elmo at the mouth of the harbour, Valette had been apprehensive about a seaward attack on his headquarters. He knew the enemy would give no quarter. He could not forget what had happened to his predecessor when a surprise attack on the inner harbour had nearly annihilated the Order, and he also remembered that it was the ability and bravery of the Maltese fishermen of Birgu and Bormla that had saved them. With the inner harbour made secure, the forts were as strong as they could ever be. The granaries were full of grain; the underground cisterns and the wells in every house that served as household reservoirs full of fresh water; and the stables full of animals.

Outside the fortresses, buildings close to the walls were levelled, wells poisoned, crops harvested or destroyed, and animals led within the walls. Now the defenders could only wait, receive the comfort of the sacraments of the Holy Church, and pray.

The Battle of St Elmo

By 20 May, the defenders were ready, while the enemy had established their main camp at Marsa. During the night of the nineteenth, the commander of one Turkish force had landed at St Thomas Bay with 3,000 men. Some skirmishes took place at Bulebel, on the outskirts of Żejtun, with cavalry and a force of about 1,000 men from Birgu harassing the raiders.

By 21 May the Turkish force had made camp on Santa Margerita heights overlooking Fort St Angelo. Mustapha Pasha and Pialì immediately started to work out a strategy. Suleiman had given them one express order: 'Destroy the Order of the Knights of Jerusalem once and for all.' A force was sent to reconnoitre the approaches to Birgu but Valette countered by sending his cavalry to attack.

The following morning Valette, standing on the walls of his citadel, gave the command and Malta woke up to the pealing of church bells. The order to 'bid the soldiers shoot' was repeated from one command post to another. The battle standard of the Order, the white cross on a red background, was unfurled on the ramparts of St Angelo. The siege had begun; the men at their posts waited for the assaults.

Mustapha and Pialì were planning. A reconnoitring party was sent out to check and test the state of readiness of Fort St Elmo. This was the result of information received from Tripoli that large reinforcements were expected from Europe. The Turkish commanders were startled at the news and realized that they had to act quickly without waiting for the arrival of Dragut, even though this went against the express instructions of the sultan. Mustapha decided that Fort St Elmo had to be captured quickly. With the fort in their hands, they would then seal off the harbour and stop reinforcements from reaching Fort St Angelo by sea. The Turkish scouting party was engaged by the defenders under Colonel Mas.

The commander-in-chief, Mustapha, set off immediately with 30 ships and 4,000 men to round the headland of Xeberras, under the menacing guns of St Elmo. He set camp on a hilly knoll and mounted heavy guns in front of the landward walls of Fort St Elmo. Gun emplacements were erected from where big guns opened fire on the fortifications.

On 24 May the battle of St Elmo began. Wave after wave of ferocious Turks attacked the ramparts only to be repulsed again and again. The battles were long and bloody and still the Turks did not gain ground while, on their part, the defenders made many sallies on the Turkish emplacements to silence the guns and to stop the enemy from bridging the moat and scaling the walls.

At the end of May, there entered on the scene the notorious corsair Dragut, the scourge of the Mediterranean. Dragut was a cunning and ferocious fighter on sea and land. He knew the shores of Malta well, having pillaged and plundered the villages at will, and often used Gozo as his base for attacks on passing ships and for replenishing his ships with water. Some Turkish commanders were getting annoyed that they were not getting anywhere, while Pialì was becoming impatient to start his final assault on Fort St Angelo before reinforcements reached the defenders. If the siege dragged on till winter, storms would wreak havoc on the fleet in the open bay of Marsaxlokk. These commanders had wisely despatched a ship to intercept Dragut and acquaint him with the desperate situation. Dragut immediately set sail for Malta with 15 ships and 1,500 men. On his arrival, Pialì's fleet set sail from Marsaxlokk and sailed past Fort St Elmo to meet him. As they were sailing past, the fort opened fire and sank one enemy ship. The combined fleet then anchored around Balluta Bay until such time as St Elmo was taken and Marsamxett harbour made safe.

The old pirate Dragut, under instructions from Suleiman to mediate between the animosities of his son-in-law Pialì and his trusted army commander Mustapha, did not like what he found on the island. He could not understand why no attempt had been made to cut off supplies and reinforcements from Sicily. He would have taken, he argued, Gozo and the north of the island first to seal off the south from any overseas help; in time the island would have capitulated of its own accord. But once the battle for St Elmo had begun, it had to be finished and won.

Dragut inspected the formidable walls and the impregnable fortifications of Forts St Angelo and St Elmo and, with the fire of an old warrior, exclaimed, 'Your plans are all wrong! You will never be able to overcome such fortified walls by a simple attack. They are too strong. Reduce them to rubble first, then make your advance, and they will fall into your hands with very little, if any, resistance.' Under Dragut's direction, the Turks surrounded St Elmo with batteries of their largest guns,

placing cannon, culverins, and basilisks on the high ground of
Mount Xeberras. Guns were also placed at Point St Anne (later
to be known as Dragut Point) to the north and on Gallows Point
(later to be known as Ricasoli Point) to the south.

The Turks started to batter and demolish the ramparts around
St Elmo, in particular a newly-constructed ravelin. The guns
pounded relentlessly, day after day, at the small fort defended
by a handful of knights and men. Time and again, Dragut judged
that the time had come for the decisive assault and sent his
janizzaries to scale the breaches; every time the defenders threw
them back. The cannon would open up again and again to
continue the continuous bombardment. The siege went on for
weeks and, by the middle of June, the pasha was starting to
lose his patience. No human being, he declared, no matter how
brave and dedicated, could withstand such punishment and he
could not understand how or why the defenders did not
surrender if any were still alive. Dragut knew well what was
keeping the defenders alive: Fort St Angelo kept sending
reinforcements and supplies across the harbour by boat under
cover of the night. So he took steps to cut off this line of
communication and supply by reinforcing the batteries on
Gallows Point and mounting culverins at the base of St Elmo to
prevent anyone landing there.

That the defenders were still alive and well, he had no doubt.
Had not the defending guns answered his own, shot for shot?
Had not the defenders repulsed each and every attack his men
made on the crumbling walls?

It was well for the defenders that Dragut did not know the true
position inside the fort. The brave defenders had been decimated,
their food was gone, and their water reduced to what they could
obtain from the night dew. Their thirst grew unbearable under
the searing June sun; their fortress walls, all but a heap of
rubble, were useless as a cover and as a line of defence, and

they were running short of ammunition. Were it not for those feeble reinforcements getting through from St Angelo by night, they would not have survived that long. Soon the knights had to accept that, with all the valour in the world, they could no more keep throwing back those endless waves of attacks. But would they give up? They felt they should, if they were given permission, fight their way out through to St Angelo, but that permission could only be given by one man - Valette himself - who insisted that St Elmo had to hold out until reinforcements reached the island.

Yet, during this attack on 18 June, a lucky shot found its mark. A cannon ball having hit the rockface near where Dragut was resting and a shrapnel hit him on the head. He died a week later. Mustapha, the commander in chief, fearing that the news would be the last straw to unnerve his troops, kept Dragut's death a secret and swore that he would personally lead a last assault on the fort. He shipped Dragut's remains to Tunis the same day.

With St Elmo cut off by land and sea, one man volunteered to solve the problem. History records that it was a valiant knight, the Commander Captain Madrona, but a solid popular tradition states it was a Maltese, the powerful swimmer Toni Bajjada, who served as a messenger between St Angelo and Mdina passing through enemy lines disguised as a Turkish soldier and swimming from Marsa up to the walls of St Angelo. Bajjada now volunteered to swim over and pass on the message of the fort's commander to the grand master, then return with the answer. At dead of night the swimmer slipped quietly into the water and started his long swim underwater, coming up only now and then to draw breath. He struck straight towards Ricasoli Point, and then cut across Kalkara Creek onto the rocks at the foot of the walls of Birgu.

From there, he ran to the landward entrance to the citadel.

Aerial view of Valletta

Showing the signet ring of knight of Aragon, Melchior de
Monserrat, who had taken over command of the fort after
Commander Broglia had been put out of action, he demanded
to be taken to the grand master to deliver the desperate message.
Valette, infuriated, could not believe that his knights,
handpicked by him to hold Fort St Elmo to the last, were now
asking permission to surrender the fort. 'No!', he declared, 'They
will not. They must not.' Then the messenger asked whether,
since the fortifications had been reduced to useless rubble and
they could hardly last another attack which was surely to come
by the following morning, they could make a final sally and try
to fight their way out? Valette's war council agreed that it was
brave common sense but the grand master opposed the idea: he
was waiting for the promised reinforcements from Sicily and
every hour that Fort St Elmo could hold on meant a ray of hope
for Malta and Christendom.

Valette's answer to the besieged garrison of St Elmo was: 'The
garrison was not to leave their post; the fort was to be held to
the last knight.' If this order was not to their liking, he, Valette,
would replace them with braver men. Then he bade the swimmer
make haste and swim back with the answer.

The twenty-second of June came and the expected attack
materialized. Monserrat rallied his men and again withstood
the terrific onslaught. The Turks, seeing their soldiers falling
one by one, retreated leaving behind 2,000 dead, while the
defenders mourned the loss of over 300 knights, Maltese, and
foreign soldiers, including Monserrat himself who was killed
by a musket shot. For the handful of defenders left there was
nothing now much left to do but hold on for as long as they
could. Their time had come. They confessed to their chaplain,
Vigneron, burned or hid all the sacred objects of the chapel,
and went to the parapets to fire their last rounds.

On 23 June the final assault on St Elmo came - as it was bound to - to a bloody end. The defenders, by now only numbering 100 in all, were reduced to mere spectres. The wounded were carried to their battle stations for the last fight where, propped up in corners, they could at least wield a broadsword and have a chance to die in arms. Once more the enemy was forced to retreat and reform. The last attack saw a sea of fierce Turks going through a breach in the walls and St Elmo fell with all knights dead or dying around the battle standard of the Order.

Mustapha, angered by the defenders' stand, ordered all survivors to be killed. Then he decided to send a message of victory to Valette and to the garrison warning them what would befall them if they resisted any longer. He ordered all dead knights to be beheaded and their heads stuck on spikes on St Elmo's battlements facing St Angelo. Their bodies were nailed to wooden crosses, crosses were slashed on their chests and, with their shields beside them as a means of identification, they were floated away towards St Angelo. There were nine of these macabre floats: five Spanish, three Italian, and one French. Francesco Balbi records their names and declares that he got the information from five Maltese soldiers who had managed to swim across to safety.

On 24 June, the eve of the feast of St John the Baptist, Valette stood on the ramparts and watched as the bodies were recovered to be given a burial befitting heroes and Christians. Then, in savage retaliation, he ordered 1,000 Turkish slaves to be beheaded and shot their heads at the enemy lines while the bodies were cast into the sea. His message was clear to one and all: 'We will fight to the last; it is better die in battle than surrender to such a fate.'

But the loss of St Elmo was, ironically, the key to Maltese victory. The delay in taking the fort proved fatal to the Turkish plans. Instead of the expected four to five days, St Elmo held out for 31 days. The loss of 109 knights and 1,500 men was more than compensated by that of 8,000 Turks and one of their principal leaders. When Mustapha entered the ruins, he could only say: 'If the daughter cost us so much, what will the price of the mother be?' By the mother, the Turkish commander meant Fort St Angelo. Two days after the fall of St Elmo, the batteries on Mount Xiberras were being transported to Corradino Hill for the attack on Fort St Michael and Fort St Angelo.

The Siege and Victory

Following the loss of St Elmo and the profanation of his knights, Valette's fury turned into a cold-blooded but calculated determination to fight on. With two fronts to defend at the same time, the walls of St Angelo and the inner-harbour defences protected by Forts St Michael and St Angelo, he immediately ordered the total clearing of land outside both forts, especially in Bormla and L-Isla, so that the attackers would have nowhere to shelter.

Mustapha had also turned his attention to these forts. The invading fleet was moved to the safe anchorage of Marsamxett harbour. Every available piece of artillery was mounted on three sites overlooking the two forts, that is Mount Xeberras and Corradino Hill, and the heights behind Birgu and Kalkara. He also moved the main body of his troops to Corradino and Sta. Margerita heights.

Mustapha, remembering the earlier strategy used at Rhodes, sent a messenger to Valette to offer an honourable surrender. Valette replied that he would only give up space in the ditches under the walls for the Turks to bury their dead in. At such an arrogant answer, Mustapha immediately started his bombardments and assaults with wave after wave of soldiers. The defenders, helped by reinforcements from Mdina, tried to impede the setting up of the Turkish camps on the high land

behind them, but by early July Birgu and Fort St Michael were
being heavily bombarded.

Such fierce attacks heralded direct assaults on these two forts,
particularly Birgu. To improve the communication between the
two forts, an idea was suggested to the grand master of floating
a pontoon between the two fortifications. Fishermen, all
excellent swimmers and good boatmen, were called upon to work
on the construction under a naval engineer known as *Iż-Żabbari*.
This structure consisted of more than 40 pontoons fastened to
each other by a chain, constituting a floating rampart and, in
an emergency, a means of despatching reinforcements from Fort
St Angelo to Fort St Michael or vice-versa. To stop, or least to
check, the landing on the beaches around L-Isla, the grand
master ordered the building of a palisade on the foreshore
around the fortifications. This work was accomplished in a few
days with the workers toiling during the night to avoid being
fired upon from Corradino.

The inner port of Marsa, from being impregnable, now became
an assault base. A number of boats from the enemy fleet
moored in Marsamxett, some authors quote about a hundred,
were dragged overland to Marsa, thus penetrating the Grand
Harbour without having to sail past Fort St Angelo. From
there they launched assaults to breach the chain boom and
the palisades. Some Turks armed with knives and hatchets
were to attack the palisades and cut down the chain so that
their fleet could get through and land an assault force against
Fort St Michael. Commander Fantone, seeing the turbaned
heads of the Turks bobbing up and down swimming towards
his command, could not make out what they were about to
do. Surely not even a mad Turk would dare swim against a
fortress! He took his time to find out but he waited too long.
The Turks had already reached the boom and were hacking
away at the only line of defence of the inner harbour where
the fleet of the Order lay.

Giuseppe Calì: Death of Dragut

(Police Academy, Floriana)

Fortunately the good fishermen of L-Isla came to the rescue. Totally disregarding the Turkish covering fire, the fishermen, almost completely naked, jumped into the sea. With knives in their mouth, they swam towards the enemy and soon put an end to the attack. Shouts turned into screams and then dead silence. It was all over very quickly, and the Maltese swam, more slowly this time, back to shore, laden with rich battle trophies, to a well-earned rest. However, there was a smile of victory on their bloodied faces but all that one could get out of *Pietru is-Sajjied* was, 'That will teach them not to swim in our creek.'

Just after this event, a Turkish officer deserted to the Christian lines. He was no common deserter, but a descendant of an ancient and noble Greek family of Lascaris with lineage going back to the Byzantine emperors. The defenders' courage and his anger at the domination of his country by the Ottoman empire made him change sides. He passed invaluable information of the Turkish intentions to the grand master and proved to be of great assistance in the defence of the island.

At the beginning of July, Hassan, king of Algiers, son of Barbarossa, arrived with 2,500 of his bravest warriors in 25 ships in aid of Pialì. On the latter's latest unsuccessful attacks on the walls of Fort St Michael, Hassan had this to say. 'I will', he rashly declared, 'storm Fort St Angelo straight away and capture it at the first attempt.' Pialì, irritated by this newly-arrived upstart, was delighted to teach such young arrogance a lesson: Hassan was put in command of an assault on L-Isla. St Angelo was Mustapha's own trophy.

At dawn on the morning of 15 July, Turkish boats came out of Marsa laden with troops led by Hassan himself. 'Such a magnificent sight of a formidable armada had never been seen', narrates Balbi, who witnessed this whole battle from his vantage point on the walls of Fort St Michael. The first wave of boats, he continued, attacked the palisades, but the musketeers on the walls opened a deadly fire, yet the enemy kept coming and eventually landed on the rocks below the walls. Hassan gave the order to scale the walls. Some made it to the top and hand-to-hand fighting ensued. A breach in the walls, caused by an explosion in a powder magazine, was also made. The Turks poured in and managed to hoist the Ottoman standard on the walls. Valette, conscious of the consequences, rushed reinforcements to the beleaguered garrison. From his observation point on Corradino, Mustapha, noticing this weakening in St Angelo's defences by this transfer of reinforcements, decided to prepare for his intended attack on the major target, Fort St Angelo. More batteries were mounted on the hills behind Kalkara thus stretching the ring of fire from Corradino heights behind the inner harbour to Kalkara. He let loose a devastating barrage on St Angelo and Senglea.

By now even the women and children of Senglea had joined in, hurling stones at and pouring cauldrons of boiling water over the attackers. Tradition says that a procession carrying the small statue of *Il-Bambina* made its way to the battlements, where it was placed facing the enemy. The fighting went on all day, but at sunset the Turkish command ordered a sudden retreat. Hassan was bewildered and forced to admit failure. His losses were enormous: some 3,000 of his men lay dead, compared to 250 of the defenders. By nightfall scores of Maltese swimmers were seen in the water fishing out rich booty from the floating Turkish bodies, richly dressed with jewels, rings, purses, and bejewelled daggers and scimitars. That night the statue was returned to the church with a bigger procession where the Sengleans gave praise and thanks to God for the deliverance of their city.

The grand master particularly thanked the knight commander, Chevalier Mesquita, and the garrison of Mdina. The commander sensing that something terrible was happening on hearing the constant rumble of gunfire and seeing a huge cloud of dust and smoke in the south, sent his favourite scout to reconnoitre. Luqa Briffa, well known for his horsemanship and audacity in crossing enemy lines, reported that the southern cities were under a fierce attack and suggested that, as a diversion, they should strike at the Turkish camp at Marsa which seemed to be guarded only by a few tired and sleepy men. The commander very wisely decided to take this opportunity and at the same time destroy the enemy's main camp and supply base. The report of the destruction at the campsite soon reached the Turkish commanders who ordered a quick retreat but by the time the retreating Turks got back all they found was death and destruction. But what angered the Turkish command most was that they had been well and truly tricked into believing that reinforcements had arrived from Sicily, as one of the escaped guards had told them.

In reprisal, Pialì led a large contingent of cavalry and foot soldiers to attack Mdina, but a cavalry sortie met the advancing force and dispersed it.

It was at this time that one attempt to land a relieving force was successful. However, it finished landing on the north-west side of the island and proceeded to march towards Mdina. A Maltese messenger from Mdina volunteered to lead the small relieving force to St Angelo. After three days they reached Kalkara creek from they were transported by boat to Birgu, entering Fort St Angelo on 5 July.

Despatches were constantly being forwarded to Don Garcia reminding him of his promise of help. As time went on, these despatches stressed more and more the urgency for reinforcements. Only some of these messages made it through the Turkish naval encirclement of the island. A number of Maltese master mariners lost their lives in volunteering to deliver these despatches to Syracuse.

But Mustapha decided to play his trump card and so teach Pialì some real battle strategy. He declared he could blast his way through into Birgu. Choosing the post defended by the langue of Castille, he ordered the digging of a mine under the walls, just as had been done at Rhodes. The defenders could hear the digging going on day and night but could not locate it exactly. The next thing they knew, they heard a loud explosion like a clap of thunder and saw stone and dust whirling in the air followed by a huge roar of applause from the Turkish side. When the dust started to clear, they saw a sea of turbans rushing through a breach in the walls and screaming dervishes wielding scimitars entering Birgu.

At first there was consternation and a sense that all was lost. The council, hastily assembled, advised the grand master to retreat into Fort St Angelo and give up Birgu to preserve and conserve the little strength they still had left. Valette gratefully acknowledged their advice but let them know that he was not going to take it. Fronting them, he asked, 'Who is with me?' and crossed the drawbridge that connected the fort to Birgu. With most of his retinue following, he ordered the bridge to be blown up. Drawing his sword, he rushed into the fray where men, women, and children were trying to stem the tide. Seeing the grand master in person among them, everyone, knights, soldiers, and Maltese, joined in with renewed vigour, and so slowly the tide started to turn with the invaders being pushed back. With the situation well in hand, Valette was asked to seek a safer place, but he refused, 'Not while the Ottoman standard flies within the walls of the city', he cried out from the clock tower. The attackers were thrown out into the ditch and their standard captured. The grand master ordered that standard to be hung in the conventual church of St Laurence. The eventful day was 7 August.

Time passed and the Turks did not advance an inch. Pialì was losing his temper and on 18 August he launched his ships and

men against St Angelo and St Michael. He could not afford
time, since supplies were running low and the army was being
decimated and suffering from disease, the oppressive heat, and
shortage of water. Moreover his ships would not withstand a
winter on the open seas. But, more than that, he received news
that an army was being assembled in Sicily. So he decided to
take over command himself over both land and sea forces. He
ordered Mustapha to surround the forts and besiege them in
preparedness for the final assault. This came on 22 August
when all gun batteries, including a new one on Salvatore heights,
opened fire on St Angelo, Birgu, St Michael, and L-Isla. It seemed
like all hell was let loose. No one could live through such
murderous bombardment, Pialì contentedly commented. But,
as darkness was falling, the standards of the Religion could
still be seen flying proudly on the battlements through the haze
of clearing smoke. Reluctantly Pialì gave orders to sound retreat.

This battle is commemorated in one of the frescoes of the siege
of Malta by Matteo Perez d'Aleccio which shows Valette, wearing
the battle vest with the cross of the Religion, sternly standing
surrounded by his knights and fighting men. With baton in
hand, he encourages his men forward to stem the hordes of
Turks rushing through the breach in the walls into the square
near the post of Castille.

At last, after a delay of three months, the army of relief, known
as the *Gran Soccorso*, finally started to arrive. A small Spanish
fleet of 28 ships and galleys with 200 knights and some 8,000
men, under Don Garcia de Toledo, left Syracuse by way of
Linosa, and approached Malta from the north-west through the
Gozo channel. On the night of 6 September, 9,000 men landed
at Mellieħa Bay. Orders were to march straight to Birgu and
thence to St Angelo, a distance of some 22 kilometres through
open country. The fleet immediately returned to Sicily to bring
more of the relieving force. Valette was understandably upset
when he learned that the force had landed so far from where it

Matteo Perez d'Aleccio: Valette wearing the battle vest

was needed, but he had felt obliged to warn them that both Marsamxett and St Paul's Bay lay in enemy hands. This meant that the only safe place for disembarkation was near Mellieħa and Valette felt he had to give the force a helping hand by attacking the enemy. It was 7 September.

With no heart in the fight, the Turkish commanders were more cautious and, after a few more skirmishes, Mustapha gave orders to strike camp and Pialì immediately set sail north. Through observation and a report by a renegade Spanish soldier that the landing force consisted only of 6,000 men, Mustapha learned that he was mistaken about the size of the relieving force. He ordered Pialì to enter St Paul's Bay and land a force of janissaries to engage the forces marching south. The succouring forces luckily had already climbed the escarpment of the Great Fault. From those heights they easily spotted the advancing Turkish force marching apparently towards Mdina. However, against the orders of King Philip of Spain, which were to march straight to the besieged cities, the relieving force, itching for a fight, rushed to attack the enemy. Although tired and discomfited, the enemy fought well, especially since the relieving forces were not as numerous as anticipated and not as disciplined. Once again the Mdina garrison came to the rescue. The governor, on learning that the friendly force were being engaged by a much larger force, sent his cavalry to join in the fray. The Turks, caught by surprise, were soon routed.

Seeing that there was no will to fight in his men, Mustapha called his troops back to ship, and everybody set sail for home to face a very disgruntled and angry Suleiman. It was 13 September.

Within a year Suleiman the Great was dead; he was succeeded by Selim II, during whose reign the Ottoman empire experienced the beginning of its decline.

Thus ended the siege of 1565 which had lasted 112 days and left behind some 30,000 of the invaders dead. The defenders mourned their losses - 250 knights and 7,000 men killed - leaving only about 600 men fit to bear arms out of the original 9,000. Some of the dead were buried in the cemetery at St Angelo. On 8 September, the garrison and people of Malta rejoiced at their signal victory and the *Te Deum* was intoned at the conventual church of St Lawrence at Birgu.

The Building of a City

Following this great victory, Birgu was renamed *Città Vittoriosa* (the victorious city), although the Maltese still fondly call by its old name. Senglea or L-Isla was honoured with the title of *Città Invicta*.

Pope Pius V offered Valette a cardinal's hat but the grand master modestly refused. He had fought as a gentleman and a warrior; he had done his duty to his Faith, to his Order, and to the people he had sworn to protect.

There is one more point worthy of mention about this siege: the part played by the women of Malta. In both L-Isla and Birgu, they showed valour beyond the call of duty and did all the work necessary to free their menfolk for actual combat. They cooked for the troops, carried the ammunition, attended the sick and the dying on the battlefield, comforted and looked after the bereaved wives and mothers and their children, and, for the first time in the Order's history, they served as nurses in the hospital. As if that was not enough, they, with their children, kept the cauldrons boiling and poured the hot tar and boiling water over the walls onto the enemy below, thus even performing some combat duty. History has a tendency to skim over all this effort by the women of Malta rather than to sing it loud and clear.

Once the siege was over, the grand master's energy and attention were directed to the building of a big and beautiful city, so long on the drawing board, which was to make Malta safe in case of another siege. Pius V sent his engineer, Francesco Laparelli, to draw a plan for its formidable walls. The building went on apace despite the lack of funds and the many difficulties presented by the uneven terrain. The kings of France, Spain, and Portugal sent some rather meagre gifts of money. The jurats of Mdina imposed a special tax and a token coinage of nominal value was struck with the Latin inscription *'non aes sed fides'* which, translated freely, means 'this is not cash but credit'. Slowly money began trickling in for this great and magnificent project, a city of palaces for the princely langues of the Order and the brave people of the island. From now on, knights and people were going to live together. Gone for ever was the idea of the collachio, the special reserve for the knights that kept them separate from the people as had been the case at Birgu.

On 28 March 1566 Valette, together with the bishop of Malta, Mgr. Cubelles, and followed by the priors, balìs, knights, and their retinues and a good part of the the people of Malta, marched to where the church of Our Lady of Victories now stands. There, after the celebration of Mass, the first stone of the new city was laid, named by the grand master 'the Most Humble City of Valletta'.

The hilly layout of Mount Xeberras presented greater problems even that those of finance. Its position, a headland between two harbours, was perfect strategically, but the amount of levelling required to accommodate a city as the designers intended was an insurmountable job in itself.

Eight thousand people worked on the project which dragged on for five years at a cost of 3,500 *scudi*. The walls of the city took another 6 years to complete. Fort St Elmo was also enlarged and greatly strengthened.

Barely had the excavations started when the scare of another Turkish invasion arose and the excavation work had to be suspended. Eventually it was discontinued because of the cost and the time involved. The result was that the levelling as completed only removed the hump of the hill, leaving sharp slopes on the sides. Those who know Valletta can feel the result as they climb its steps and steep rises of the streets which run at right-angles to the main street, now called Republic Street, and slope sharply down to the sea.

One piece of excavation in the whole project is worth noting. The knights, anxious to have a safe place for their galleys just like they had in the idyllic island of Rhodes, wanted to excavate an inner harbour for their smaller craft which was known as *mandreki*, from a Greek word meaning 'a keep for sheep'. They therefore called the little harbour in Malta *manderaggio* (in Maltese *mandraġġ*). But the job of quarrying into the rock below sea level proved too difficult and the project was abandoned. However, a regulation had been imposed that only stone from the *manderaggio* was to be used for house-building in Valletta. The work kept on going until 4 metres above sea level but then it was completely abandoned and never actually connected to Marsamxett waters. All sort of nonsense has been written about this place. People who have never seen the *mandraġġ* say it was the underground of Malta and a place to keep away from, a very unsafe place to wander about by oneself. In reality it was a densely-populated depressed area of about two acres lying at a lower level than the surrounding quarters. Its inhabitants were boatmen and watermen, rough but hard-working men no different from any other. After the Second World War the *mandraġġ* was knocked down and replaced by blocks of flats.

By 1571, Valletta had progressed sufficiently for the Convent (as the central body of the Order was called) to move from Birgu, but this transfer had to be carried out by Valette's successor, del Monte.

The Church of Our Lady of Victories

Monument to Grand Master Valette at St John's

(St John's Church, Valletta)

Valette, old and tired, frustrated by delays in the his pet project, died on 21 August 1568, after a short illness. He was without any doubt the most illustrious grand master of the Order. His feats as a warrior, administrator, and builder carved for him an immortal name in history. Buried at the church of Our Lady of Victories, his remains were later transferred to the crypt of the conventual church of St John's.

'And to the eternal memory of the most illustrious Brother Jean Valette, Frenchman, who after a great number of various memorable deeds, done with courage and success, near Tripoli in Africa, and in Numidia as well as in Greece, on sea and on land, by unanimous consent of the whole Order elected Master and Chief, increased so much the high opinion he enjoyed for a very long time, that in 1565, when the Christian princes hesitated and played for time, he saved Malta besieged by Suleiman, saved the old city and the castles, drove all the Turks out of the island, purged the two seas from pirates, and constructed with incredible speed and admirable art the new city of Valletta, a sure bulwark against the enemy of our faith and eternal monument to the name of Valette and to the French name. He died on 21 August 1568, on the same date that he had become grand master eleven years before.

Terrible facing the enemy, and dear to his people, he deserved so long a life. So great a memory of so great a man, and so powerful an example of courage for the soldiers of Jerusalem were all buried into this ground.'

Thus says the epitaph on the tomb of Grand Master Valette in the crypt of St John's in Valletta. He was 73 years and 6 months old.

Two days later, on 23 August 1568, the Order elected its forty-ninth grand master.

Pietro del Monte

1568-72

Pietro del Monte, prior of Capua and the valiant commander of Senglea during the siege, was elected grand master on 23 August 1568.

Del Monte had an outstanding reputation, having been appointed in his younger days by the pope as governor of Castel Sant'Angelo, the immediate line of defence of the Holy See. For years before the great siege, the Turkish fleet, under the command of Dragut, had infested the two seas, as the west and east Mediterranean were called. In 1558, del Monte took over the command of the fleet and chased Dragut who had been attacking Malta and Gozo whenever he needed water or whenever it suited him. Del Monte took it in hand to stop these raids and accomplished it with a good measure of success. He was so highly qualified that, without any hesitation, his brothers-in-arms elected him within two days of Valette's demise. Del Monte immediately threw himself into the task of

Grand Master Pietro del Monte

finishing the building of Valletta. There was peace over the land and some money was trickling in.

But idle time was making itself felt amongst the knights. The grand master, immersed in the intricacies of building a city, neglected to engage his knights in either civil or military matters. This inactivity amongst the most ambitious knights found an outlet in corsairing activities. They took it on themselves to set sail on their own, some asking permission afterwards, while others did not even bother, and chase any floating craft they laid eyes on. These self-made captain-pirates, after a few days at sea, returned to their home-port laden with booty. Any ship not flying the flag of the Religion was fair game if it looked a good and easy prey.

Such a state of affairs could not last for long. It could not be tolerated, especially by the Order's arch-enemy, the Turks, who were just as determined to destroy the knights. Eventually the tide started to turn. In 1570, two Maltese galleys were shipwrecked and three others fell to the Turks. Selim II, who had just succeeded Suleiman the Magnificent, took heart and started preparations for another attack on Malta, after having ousted the Venetians from Cyprus. After the disaster of the siege, Selim still had all the money needed for the venture. These rumours of another invasion made the Order rally and prepare for another onslaught. The work on the city was slowed down and work was diverted to the outer fortifications.

The Order rallied so well to the call for the defence of the island that the different langues got in each other's way in trying to outdo one another. Unfortunately the old rivalries started coming back to the fore.

Meanwhile, Selim's threat of invasion did not materialize and the numerous knights, all huddled together on the claustrophobic island, gave vent to their pent-up energy in street fights amongst themselves. Many a battle took place with dead and wounded being left in the streets. A weary and disillusioned grand master, seeing all these setbacks to his pet project and still suffering from the loss of three of his galleys in a naval battle against the famous corsair Ucciali, begged Pius V to relieve him of his post and he respectfully sent in his resignation.

The pope immediately refused to accept it. Del Monte was told to put his house in order by paying more attention to the needs of his men than to the building of the new city. Del Monte saw his error in not getting his knights engaged in designing and supervising the construction of the city and immediately put into practice this idea of getting them involved. As a first step, he moved the Convent from Birgu to Valletta. On 18 March 1571, with great pomp and pageantry, the transfer of the seat of government took place.

The grand master started to build his palace on a piece of land in the centre of the city where his uncle had already built a wooden house, as a gesture of encouragement to others to buy land and move to the new city. This land had been bought, it is said, from the noble family of Xiberras on perpetual leasehold on the payment of five grains of wheat a year and a glass of water from a well on the property. There is indeed a mouth to a well at the entrance to the corridor leading to the Throne Room which was renamed as the Hall of St Michael and St George during the British administration.

This location for the Magistral Palace went against the wishes of the council who favoured the spot where the Auberge de Castille now stands and where the Maltese architect, Gerolamo Cassar, had previously planned it. However, it was Cassar again who prepared the plans for new palace which was completed by Grand Master la Cassiere. Work on the auberges was also started, seven of them to Cassar's plans. Aragon was the first to be built, followed by Provence, with its chapel, the church of

Architect Gerolamo Cassar

St Barbara; Italy with its magnificent chapel, the church of St Catherine; Castille and Leon; Germany, later demolished to make way for the Anglican cathedral of St Paul, and France, which was demolished by enemy action in the Second World War and is the site of the General Workers Union headquarters.

At this time also, the Dominican friars asked the grand master for some land in order to build a church to be able to look after the spiritual needs of the inhabitants of the new city; up to now these needs were being administered by the parish of Qormi from a church (now known as Sta. Lucia) in the new city. The site was granted on 10 April 1571, and a church and convent were built on plans by Gerolamo Cassar. Pius V confirmed it as the first parish church of the new city the following year under the title of *Beata Vergni ta' Portu Salvu* (The Blessed Virgin of Porto Salvo). He also encouraged the building of a church and convent for the Friars Minor, known as *Ta' Giesu*.

In actual fact the move from Birgu had the reverse effect to that intended. The knights were not interested in engineering and did very little to help in the construction of the city. There was very little accommodation to provide them with the life they were accustomed to; for instance, the grand master's palace consisted of only two rooms and a hall. One great decision was taken to keep discipline within the Convent: a decision that helped change world history - the grand master bid his fleet join the fleets of Spain, Genoa, Venice, and the Papal States to engage the Turkish enemy at Lepanto in the Gulf of Corinth on 7 October 1571. Eventually, after much fierce fighting, the Christian Holy League's victory was complete and the disaster that befell the Ottoman navy is indicated, rightly or wrongly by many historians, as the beginning of the end of the Ottoman empire.

Pietro del Monte died on 27 January 1572. His body was interred in the church of Our Lady of Victories and was later transferred to the crypt of St John's.

Jean L'Eveque de la Cassiere

1572-81

Jean L'Eveque de la Cassiere was born in 1503. Another Frenchman, his name was not unknown in the annals of the Order's naval history. Well-known for his valour and leadership, he was promoted to the langue of Auvergne's highest position - that of grand marshal.

La Cassiere was, perhaps, the luckiest grand master to start with, and yet, his reign finished as the most miserable and troublesome in the history of the Order. In between these periods, he gave so much to the Order and to the Maltese.

The first years of his reign were peaceful ones: Selim II's threat to attack the island never materialized. La Cassiere took advantage of this period of peace and began to devote most of his time and money to building the greatest of all monuments of the Order, the conventual church of St John, the crowning glory of Valletta. He chose the Maltese architect Gerolamo Cassar to design his magnificent church to the glory of God

Grand Master Jean l'Eveque de la Cassiere

and the honour of the Order. In this church he later ordered the re-burial of the remains of Grand Masters L'Isle Adam, d'Omedes, la Sengle, and Valette. And to show the great respect the Order had towards another illustrious knight, the remains of the 'humble knight' Sir Oliver Starkey, Valette's adviser and secretary, were also interred in the crypt of the grand masters.

The long and vaulted interior of the church was originally as austere as the fa ade still is. The side altars were allotted as chapels to the different langues: Baviere, Provence, France, Italy, Germany, Auvergne, Aragon, and Castille and Portugal. The embellishment of the church was undertaken by successive grand masters.

Gerolamo Cassar had helped to build the fortifications of Valletta which still look as formidable today as they did then. He also designed the auberges, including the Auberge d'Auvergne, which was used as the law courts and which was destroyed in the Second World War; the Auberge de Provence, a most stately palace which happily withstood the German bombs and which today houses the National Museum of Archaeology; and the Auberge de France, which was demolished by bombs in 1942. Then there was the austere Auberge d'Aragon, which from 1921 to 1932 served as the official residence to the prime minister of the Maltese government, and the beautiful auberge of Italy with its chapel dedicated to St Catherine of Siena, just off Castille Place.

But the most splendid of them all was re-built later - the Auberge de Castille. This opulent building was refurbished by Grand Master Pinto and displays a magnificent fa ade. It housed the Castilian and Portuguese knights in splendour and richness matched, possibly, only by that of Provence. The English auberge was not to be built in Valletta, the langue having been suppressed by Henry VIII a few years after the Order settled in Malta. The presence of English knights ceased to exist with

The conventual church of St John, exterior

the death of Sir Oliver Starkey and his two other English companions who were killed in the siege.

The langue of Germany did have a small auberge which was demolished in 1858 to make way for the building of St Paul's Anglican cathedral. During the reign of Grand Master Rohan, the English and German langues were amalgamated by the consent of George III of England and Prince Charles, the elector of Bavaria, in 1782. The Anglo-Bavarian langue was housed in an auberge on the lower end of the city near St Elmo, more commonly known as the 'Baviere'. After 1921, the building served for some time as a secondary school (called the 'Central') for boys.

Another notable building is the Sacred Infirmary, the hospital of the Order, overlooking St Elmo and St Lucy bastion. With all

The conventual church of St John, interior

Auberge de Castille, Valletta

The Sacred Infirmary

its warlike attitudes and other preoccupations, the Order never forgot the purpose for which it had been brought into being. Grand Master la Cassiere made certain that in his new city there must be a centre for the charitable work of the hospitallers. The sacred infirmary was meant for those sick individuals, friend or foe, who needed their care. The infirmary was designed to be the largest and the most elegant and efficient then in existence, and the envy of the rest of Europe. The site chosen lay at the entrance to one of the most picturesque harbours in the world. For security it had Fort St Elmo in front and a bastion, St Lucy bastion, with some 70 metres of sheer drop to the water's edge and which ran the full length of the hill down to Lascaris Gate The site unfortunately suffers from the inclement weather when the gregale blows. The infirmary was later greatly enlarged by the brothers Cotoner and won such a professional reputation that patients with no connection with the Order came for treatment from far and wide. The hospital lay under the jurisdiction of the langue of France, and its importance within the Order was measured by the fact that the grand hospitaller was the second senior dignitary after the grand master.

The building, after extension, is about 170 metres long and 12 metres wide and was at one time the longest hall in Europe. This is the only part of the hospital which is T-shaped. The building is in three levels: the top or main ward where patients ate off silver plate; the level below, known as second level, was a ward for mental cases; while galley slaves occupied the lower or third level. Well-trained nurses were employed to assist the medical and surgical staff. This institution was the first to adopt the sterilization of surgical instruments.

To each langue was allotted a particular day to attend to the sick when each member, in all humility, had to take his turn. The patients were fed well: 200 fowls were used daily for chicken broth alone. Some of silver plate used by patients can still be seen at the National Museum of Fine Arts but most were melted down by Napoleon into 3,500 lbs. of bullion to pay his troops in the Egyptian campaign. The medications were kept in magnificent majolica jars and the patients were accommodated one to a bed, a first of its kind for Europe. As in Birgu, no arrangement for the hospitalization for women was contemplated. The old infirmary at Mdina was, as it had done before 1530, to take care of female medical needs. After the Order left the island, the infirmary fell into disuse until later the British transferred the hospital to a new building in Floriana. During the First World War, it was again used as a military hospital for the wounded of the Gallipoli campaign. Later uses of the *Sacra Infirmeria* were many, including the headquarters for the Malta police. The building was severely damaged during the Second World War but has since been finely restored, this time as a conference centre.

So far everything had gone well for la Cassiere, with beautiful buildings going up and peace all around him. This aura of peace created jealousy amongst the princes of Europe who began to foment trouble for him. Moreover, this good grand master, seeing that free-thinking in Europe was capturing the minds of his young knights, invited the Holy Inquisition to Malta. This, unfortunately, would start a whole series of troubles and disquiet over the land and signalled the second phase of his reign, the troublesome one.

Troubled Times of la Cassiere

La Cassiere had more than his share of troubles with the bishop on the one hand, and the inquisitor, whom he had introduced, to the on the other. The post of inquisitor in Malta was considered an important one, as the men who headed it were usually clerics of high distinction. Of the 60 inquisitors appointed, 25 were subsequently elevated to the rank of cardinal, and two ultimately became popes, that is, Alexander

VII and Innocent XII. Many held episcopal rank. The first inquisitor was Bishop Pietro Dusina sent by Pope Gregory XIII as an intermediary between him and the bishop of the island.

To complicate matters for poor la Cassiere, the pope and the kings of France and Spain assumed the right to make appointments for priories situated in their respective territories, depriving the Order of overall authority and autonomy. Priors and even lesser officers, externally stationed, owed or transferred their allegiance and loyalty from their sovereign grand master to their respective sovereign king who now dispensed promotions and new appointments at his will and pleasure. This situation signalled an excuse to the Spanish knights to rebel against the French-dominated council regardless of their grand master. To the Spanish knights this was their last chance to minimize the power of France over Malta and the Order by fostering a revolt to replace their lawful grand master with a Spanish one. In order to conceal their real aim, they chose a hapless and intriguing man as the head of the revolt.

Romegas, a knight commander and a renowned fighter of the 1565 siege, saw his chance of becoming the next grand master, and accepted to lead the revolt which actually broke out in 1578. Things really got out of control and the grand master, beset by troubles on all sides, had to resort to outside help. He found he could trust no one around him; he had become a pawn in the hands of foreign princes and was being manipulated by his knights like a puppet on a string.

La Cassiere decided to seek the intervention of Gregory XIII. The pope, who did not want to compromise his precarious position with either France or Spain, decided against sending a direct representative. He sent instead the archbishop of Palermo to try to re-establish peace within the Order. This mission

Pope Gregory XIII

completely failed as it was destined to from the beginning, the
bishopric of Palermo being another Spanish court appointment.
It had another disastrous result on the Maltese population. They
now became subject to three separate jurisdictions: the Order,
the curia (the bishop of Malta, Mgr. Royas), and the inquisition
(Mgr. Dusina), so they could hardly stand any more interference
from yet another quarter.

Despite the efforts of the pope as intermediary between the
two camps, the rebellious knights succeeded in grabbing power.
The grand master was placed under house arrest in his own
palace, then unceremoniously locked up in Fort St Angelo like
a common criminal. The one man who had never wronged
anyone, who had given so much of himself and of his personal
riches for the common good, was now being labelled as a evildoer
and publicly disgraced. Neither of the new appointments of
bishop of Malta, Mgr. Gargallo, nor the inquisitor, Cefalotto,
raised a finger to help the legitimate authority or to quell the
unrest, nor did they help the pope's representative in his efforts
to restore peace.

And now that the knights were at each other's throats, this
discontent did not stop within the Order. The Maltese nobles,
in their enclave of Mdina, were rather pleased that the authority
of the grand master was being attacked publicly. Taking
advantage of the situation, they clandestinely aided and abetted
the rebellious Spanish knights, that is, the side which owed the
same allegiance as them. The nobles could never stomach the
arrogant knights, neither would they submit to the Order's
authority voluntarily. The nobles' allegiance was to the king
of Spain whom they considered their rightful liege, even
though he had failed them and had betrayed them to the Order
in 1530.

On the other hand, the commercial class was enjoying an
unprecedented boom in the peace that reigned during the early

years of la Cassiere's rule. The fortune that this man was spending on building the new city and his beloved conventual church of St John's had created work for everyone. The many other ongoing projects all led to increased prosperity. And now these upstart Spanish knights had to cause trouble and upset the peace! Even at the best of times, the man in the street could never stomach Spanish arrogance and their ascetic way of life. The common man could not condone the absolute right of kings, especially when such kings impertinently sold them as serfs. Had they not ransomed back their land with all their worldly possessions, even down to their wedding rings? And, this same God-fearing sovereign, after having himself sworn that Malta would never be sold again, ceded their island to the Order.

Casting their eyes around, on the other hand, they saw the good life and the radical thinking of the French, with riches flowing even to them and not just to the Convent and its courtiers. The business people rather liked and approved of the French grand master and his generous attitude towards them. At the end it came to the aristocracy on one side and the business world on the other, with the worker following his master.

Meanwhile la Cassiere was brought to trial and accused of all sorts of crimes that he never could possibly have committed. These accusations could not be proved and Romegas was forced to capitulate. Although la Cassiere was reinstated, by now he had suffered enough all. With resignation in mind, he set sail for Rome on 14 September in the midst of a storm.

Romegas, seeing that things were going wrong for him, also set off immediately for Rome and arrived there before la Cassiere but was completely ignored. On the other hand, la Cassiere received a tumultuous welcome. In his progress to the Holy City, 800 knights headed his procession and a number of cardinals followed him, while all through his progress to the

La Cassiere's monument at St John's

(St John's Church, Valletta)

The Magistral Palace

pope's presence, he was surrounded by princes of different kingdoms.

Romegas did not like what he saw. The pope received la Cassiere with all the pomp and pageantry of a sovereign. Romegas, unwilling to bear the shame of being looked upon as a traitor, committed suicide.

And yet the rebellious knights in Malta refused to accept la Cassiere as their lawful grand master.

Just at this juncture, death stepped in and settled the dispute. La Cassiere died in Rome on 21 December 1581, at the age of 78. La Cassiere's great monument is the conventual church of St John's which he built out of his own money and which includes the crypt where his remains now lie right beneath the high altar. He finished the Magistral Palace, started by del Monte, at his own expense (although this was greatly enlarged by later grand masters), and other magnificent buildings, that 'his brothers might enjoy the good life'. He was a rigid but an honest and upright man. His character was typical of the old soldier that he was: uncompromising, and not well tuned to the changing times. He may have been tactless but he was lovingly remembered. Pope Gregory honoured la Cassiere by writing the epitaph of this kind and generous grand master.

Hughes de Verdalle

1581-95

The death of la Cassiere somehow seemed to satisfy both sides, and for a time the Order experienced internal peace. Henry III of France, however, declared his outrage by the untimely death of such an illustrious son of France. To think that so glorious a reign, as la Cassiere's, had to come to such an abrupt and despicable end because of a rabble of Spanish and Italian knights, was an affront to him personally and to his country. 'Such culprits, such upstarts, such rebels against lawful authority must be brought to justice and punished,' was Henry's outcry. Nothing less would serve as reparation to the memory of la Cassiere. The pope and the king of Spain tried to placate the aggrieved king. They pointed out that there was peace now between the langues of France and those of Spain, so why stir trouble again? The past was past and it was better to let things be. But Henry was adamant that, if reparations were not forthcoming, he would split the Order by recalling all the French knights and establish the langues of France on French territory, in Provence.

Grand Master Hughes de Verdalle

The pope understood that the king of France was showing off his anger to give the Spanish knights a bad name and ensure the election of a French candidate to the magistracy. The pope, therefore, calmed this kingly wrath by submitting for consideration three French names to the council as candidates for the succession. And so, on 12 January 1592, Hughes de Loubenx-Verdalle was elected as grand master. Verdalle had been la Cassiere's comrade-in-arms.

The pope had played his cards well. Verdalle, with his gentle manner, had already won the respect of everyone, and with his good character and his love of life, ensured for himself a universally-acclaimed election. Although Verdalle was a Frenchman, he could rally the sympathy and allegiance of all the langues. It seemed that Verdalle's reign was going to begin and continue in peace.

And so it would have been, had not the French court been so envious and bent on causing trouble, even to a compatriot. France still insisted on its demands that the rebellious knights be punished. The new grand master took the matter in his hands: the culprits were brought to justice and given a light sentence. Thus all sides were satisfied and at last peace could reign over the land.

Verdalle's first years were ones of grandeur. The grand master implored Clement VIII to have the Jesuit Order establish and administer a university of studies on the island. He also asked the pope to send the Capuchin fathers. To satisfy the wishes of the latter Order of monks, he granted them a piece of land outside the city walls on a hill (now known as Crucifix Hill) overlooking the Marsa and the heights of Corradino on the other side of the harbour and nominated Gerolamo Cassar in charge of the project of building their church and convent. He also took care of his brother knights. The good grand master built a large building, opposite the sacred infirmary, to house those knights who wanted to retire to a life of prayer and contemplation. This was called the *Camerata* after a Jesuit priest who looked after their spiritual needs. He also took care of those who misbehaved, by building a new jail in St Dominic Street, Valletta.

Of his monuments, the one that he will always be remembered by, the vast square palace built on a bluff on the outskirts of Rabat, overlooking the lush valley of Boschetto. Verdalle Palace, his three-storeyed villa fortress, is martial and feudal in its aspect with its high and mighty walls, secret walkways, and sharp-angled battlement towers at each corner. The whole building is surrounded by a moat, from where the creamy stone for the whole structure was quarried. On entering this palace, there is a great barrel-vaulted living room where Verdalle dallied in luxury with his friends. Such a life of splendour naturally created envy and made him enemies. Rumours started to go round that the pious brother should rather attend to his devotions than cavort in such opulence.

The building of this palace created work for all those who wanted to work and the people of the island were very happy. Designed by Cassar, it had a flat roof (which was later surrounded by a baroque balustrade by Grand Master Vilhena) reached by a beautiful circular staircase. From the roof, one can survey almost all of Malta and Gozo. One can also look down over the only woodland on the island, the Boschetto or *Il-Buskett*, a true oasis of greenery in a dry and rocky land. The motto inscribed over the doors reads *Ros et Pluvia Monte Verdala* (May dew and rain fall on Mount Verdalle). In the valley there are terraces of orange, loquat, and other fruit trees. Following the stream down the valley, there is another venerable spot, a sharp contrast to the haughty structure high on the bluff. This is a humble shack which had been built by Valette as his hunting·lodge.

This 'Little Forest' was the country retreat of Verdalle where

Verdalle Palace

Grand Master Verdalle wearing the red *biretta* and Cardinal's robe
(National Museum of Fine Arts, Valletta)

he and his friends delighted in the good things of life, the glory and the power. However, rumours of the goings-on grew stronger and more damning so that, by 1587, that the Order was becoming embarrassed, to say the least.

Verdalle repaired to Rome where he was received with great honours, usually bestowed on reigning monarchs. And the pope, sensing where the rumours were coming from, and to balance the power of the inquisition, created Verdalle a 'prince of the church' by bestowing on him the cardinal's hat. In great pomp, Cardinal Grand Master Verdalle returned to Malta. Both the pope and the grand master believed that this would stop all seditious rumours.

But fate took a different turn: plague broke out on the island. It was so severe and widespread that all quarrelling was forgotten. The plague hit hard both city and country, affecting both rich and poor. The city gates were closed, and also Birgu and L-Isla were cut off from the rest of the island. Processions and devotions to St Roque, protector from the plague, were held in every parish. Gozo suffered tremendous losses and was

The tomb of Grand Master Verdalle
(St John's Church, Valletta)

reduced to a veritable desert. Once the plague was over, life went on as usual: Verdalle and his court resumed the good life and old rivalries resurfaced.

Out of concern for his people, Verdalle sought to create work on the island by adding new fortifications to Fort St Angelo. The bickering within the Order grew into open insults to the grand master. Verdalle, by now a sexagenarian, became a tired and sceptical man. Discontented with life around him and surrounded by open confrontation, he once again retreated to Rome, where he died at the age of 64 on 4 May 1595. His body was brought back to Malta for burial in the crypt of St John's. Ever magnanimous to his death, he was the only one who bequeathed in full all his worldly goods to the Order.

Martin Garzes

1595-1601

Martin Garzes of the langue of Aragon was elected as the tenth grand master to reign over Malta on 8 June 1595. With no intervention from popes or kings, the Spanish knights succeeded in placing on the throne once again one of their own. The French knights had become indifferent and even wary of France's intrusion in the affairs of the Order. Both factions seemed content to lie low and allow a peaceful spell to their new 70-year-old grand master. This peace bore fruit for it brought abundance to the land.

During Garzes' five-year reign, the treasury burst with money, so much so that for the first time ever, all taxes were rescinded. The Order exuded confidence and competence. The knights felt that they were leaders of nations, secure in their little island nation. This prosperity urged the young knights to venture far afield not only in pursuit of booty but also of battle honours, as when they flocked to the aid of Hungary against the Turks. The grand master encouraged this movement and helped both

Grand Master Martin Garzes

Grand Master Fra Martin Garzes's monument

(St John's Church, Valletta)

financially and materially, thus ensuring that his knights had their hands full and that they spent their energy against the enemy. He also recruited men from outside the Order, including Swiss nationals of noble descent. These battlefield recruits and their riches were accepted from anyone, Catholic or not. All that was necessary to buy an entry into the brotherhood was to show proof of some Catholic ancestors who had been legitimately married.

With such a buoyant treasury, Garzes paid attention to works of charity. He established an institution to redeem Christian slaves, the *Monte di Redenzione* (a foundation for the redemption of slaves). He also set up another foundation, the *Monte di Pietà*, to help those in need of ready cash, by lending money at very favourable interest, against the pawning of personal goods such as clothing or jewellery.

Garzes enjoyed peace as no other grand master had, and in his old age he wanted nothing to upset it, even going to the point of disregarding the inquisition's encroachment on the jurisdiction of the Order. The grand master gave in on almost all points for the sake of keeping the peace. Unfortunately this was the signal to the inquisition that it had come to Malta to stay and be a major influence in the running of the island and a power in the land. The new inquisitor, Del Bufalo, raised and introduced new claims thus slowly but surely diminishing the grand master's authority. But Garzes' reign began and ended in peace. Peacefully and rather unnoticed, he passed away at the age of 74 on 6 February 1601. He is buried in St John's. His grave bears what is perhaps the shortest epitaph of all.

At the beginning of his magistracy, Garzes wanted to establish a seat of learning under the direction of the Society of Jesus, better known as the Jesuits. On the advice of Bishop Gargallo, the Jesuits set up a college which was later to become the university of Malta.

Alof de Wignacourt

1601-22

At the turn of the century, the Order was rising high on the crest of great achievements, peace at home and riches on battle-fields abroad. With old Garzes gone, the knights looked around for a leader who would continue his style of government. They did not have to look far. Alof de Wignacourt, a descendant of the illustrious Dutch family of Picardy, had all the marks of leadership. He had proved himself on the battlefield where, at the tender age of 17, he had fought as a volunteer in the siege of 1565 under Valette himself. His valour, courage, and prudence earned for him the coveted knighthood. He was elected grand master.

Immediately Wignacourt set out to restore the Order to its original vigour. Within a year of his election, he set out to attack and defeat the Muslims on African shores and at Patras in 1603. The Order's storming of Turkish strongholds and their seizing of Turkish ships and slaves, enraged the sultan. In 1605, swearing to annihilate the Order once and for all, the sultan sent an armada of 60 galleys to attack the island. The Turkish

Grand Master Alof de Wignacourt

fleet sailed by way of Gozo, hugging the land to avoid detection.
It made land near Balluta Bay and managed to land 5,000 men
in open country.

But the island was by now well-prepared to deal with marauding
corsairs as knights and natives were more than ready to deal
with the intruders. By nightfall the defenders were chasing the
Turks back to their ships, and by the following morning there
was nothing left to remind the knights and the Maltese of the
Turkish attack.

The strengthening of the island defences was well justified.
From the very beginning of his election, Wignacourt started to
build fortifications along the coast. He built towers at Dragunara
Point and St George's, to the north of Marsamxett, armed with
four guns; a tower with two guns to defend St Paul's Bay; and
another tower with four guns at Qawra. A tower and a battery
of six guns were sited on Madliena hill to guard the shores in
between. To the south of the Grand Harbour, he built Fort St
Thomas with a battery of six guns to protect the bay. This bay
was very popular with Turkish corsairs, the latest incursion by
a fleet of 60 ships having taken place in 1614 prior to the building
of the fort. The grand master also built an even stronger fort,
Fort St Lucian, to protect Marsaxlokk Bay, which was later
commissioned by Rohan.

Wignacourt had by now consolidated the security of his domain
and shown his might to foe and friend alike. In the ensuing
peace and with an overflowing treasury, he turned his attention
to the better things of life. His main object was to bring a good
water supply to Valletta. Utilizing all unemployed labour, he
built the famous aqueduct from outside Mdina to the palace
square in Valletta.

While Wignacourt was engaged chasing and fighting the Turks
and preoccupied with creating work for the people, the

Fort St Lucian, at Marsaxlokk

The Monumental Arch, built in 1739, in front of the Aqueduct,
erected in 1615 by Grand Master Alof de Wignacourt

inquisition, under Mgrs. Diotallevi and Corbara, had almost a free hand on the island. However, with the return of Wignacourt's attention to the affairs of government, problems between the inquisition and the government multiplied and pressures started to mount. The inquisition managed to create unrest between the langues and some knights revolted against the grand master after two knights were sentenced to death by hanging for murder by Inquisitor Carbonese.

Wignacourt, with the enigmatic charm of a born leader, managed to calm the rebellious knights and peace was restored. In 1622 the grand master sent the galleys of the Order to join the French fleet against the Huguenots. Old Wignacourt, still an energetic man and a lover of the hunt, got sunstroke while hunting and passed away on 14 September 1622.

The old warrior, the last of the 1565 fighters, had lived to a ripe old age of 75. He had proved that a mighty empire could be checked, and even repulsed. He planned the defence of the island to ensure domestic security, while fighting the enemy abroad. He completed the fortifications of Valletta and built a number of coastal watch towers. It was the signals from these towers that saved Malta from the Turkish attack of 1605. Starting from one tower, the watch which spotted the enemy, the signal of 'enemy in sight' was passed to the watch towers on either side by lighting a bonfire. These towers then lit their own bonfires to relay the message to the next tower. In this way the island could be alerted in a trice.

Wignacourt's greatest achievement in civil works was certainly the bringing of water to Valletta for which he mostly paid out of his own pocket. By means of gravity, an aqueduct brought water from Il-Fawwara, on the Dingli-Rabat plateaux to Valletta, a distance of some 15 kilometres. It starts from springs coming out of a rock cave from where water is carried underground to Attard where it then flows into an aqueduct until Hamrun.

Wignacourt Fountain in Treasury Street, Valletta

Wignacourt Tower in Floriana

From there the water flows again underground to Floriana and on to a fountain in Treasury Square, Valletta. It was completed after five-and-half years of toil in April 1615. This date is recorded on the tower erected at the entrance to Argotti Gardens.

In his fight against the intrusion of the inquisition, Wignacourt received for himself and his successors the title of 'Prince of the Holy Empire' from Emperor Charles of Spain in 1607. His troubles with the inquisition were doubled by quarrels with Bishop Cagliares who wanted to move his residence from Mdina to Valletta but Wignacourt objected to the building of an episcopal palace in his city. The pope, to whom the dispute was referred, decided that the building of the palace could go ahead provided that it contained no dungeons, as these would in effect be giving the bishop the right of criminal jurisdiction in the capital of the island. Cagliares was indignant and he immediately wrote to Rome accusing the grand master of wanting to rule as a monarch over the island and that he was insisting that clerics performed coastguard duty. These three-cornered disputes amongst grand master, bishop, and inquisitor went on almost to the end of the Order's reign over the island.

The common man loved their *sultan*. His presence at their festivities was greatly appreciated especially the *Imnarja* races. He built a gallery at the top the road then leading to Rabat from where he distributed the *palju* (the winner's banner) to the winner of the race, After the races the multitude of people would gather at *Il-Buskett* by Verdala Palace celebrating St John's eve with singing and dancing and eating.

In 1612 the general chapter issued a decree forbidding the sale of books belonging to deceased knights, as apparently the decree of 1555 was being ignored. However, there was as yet no attempt to form a library.

Wignacourt lies buried in St John's.

Luis Mendes de Vasconcellos

1622-23

After Wignacourt's 23-year-long magistracy, foreign wars, and fast building projects, and good living at home, the Order seemed to need someone who could slow everything down for a while to consolidate what had been achieved and perhaps work on ways to stop the squabbling between the Order, the Church, and the inquisition.

The knights found this man in Luis Mendes de Vasconcellos, the Portuguese-born balì of Acre and a member of the langue of Castille. An old man of quiet disposition, prudence, and wisdom, he was accepted and hailed by all sides. His great legislative experience gave a hope of big changes in reconciling the Maltese people and their *Università* with the Order's administration. But that was not to be. Overcome by his age, he survived only seven months. He died on 7 March 1623 and was buried in St John's.

His attitude to life can be summarized from his portrait. On

Grand Master Luis Mendes de Vasconcellos

The Monument of Grand Master Fra Luis Mendes de Vasconcellos

(St John's Church, Valletta)

the table beside him were depicted the crucifix and books of devotion and not the emblems of sovereignty as with other grand masters. This grand master's death also saw the passing of the era of greatness in valour on the battlefield and service to mankind for which the Order was a beacon to the civilized world.

Antoine de Paule

1623-36

In his last hours, the good Vasconcellos recommended a knight from Toulouse as his successor. Antoine de Paule had contested the grandmastership against Vasconcellos but the latter had won by quite a large margin. Born in Gascony in 1552, de Paule came from an ancient and illustrious family that had always shown great loyalty to the crown of France and was well versed in court procedure and jurisdiction.

As a true descendant of such a noble family, de Paule introduced patterns of behaviour normally found in royal courts, rather than in such austere surroundings as that of the Order of St John. The Order at first had a long string of Spanish grand masters who shared strong ideas of absolute rule. By now grand masters were slowly changing from soldier-saints into imitations of 'his most holy Catholic majesty', and slowly but surely obliterating in all but name the ancient privileges of the Maltese.

141

Grand Master Antoine de Paule

With de Paule, life at court began to change until it became
quite complex and ceremonial. For instance, persons who
desired to be received by his most eminent highness had to
present themselves wearing a silk shirt and English gloves.
The grand master's titles became longer and longer and more
high-sounding. A new era had begun in the life at the court
of the most eminent and most reverend lord, monsignor, grand
master of the sacred religion and most illustrious Order of
the Hospital and of the Holy Sepulchre in Jerusalem, prince
of Malta, Gozo, and Rhodes, and lord of the royal domain of
Tripoli. Such were the titles grand masters were now
bestowing upon themselves.

The soft living at the headquarters of the Order may be said to
have begun with de Paule. He built a palace surrounded by
most beautiful gardens of orange trees and flowers with lovely
water fountains to keep the air cool. This garden at Attard,
right in the middle of the island, he named after his patron
saint, 'San Anton'. The living in this palace and gardens was
unsurpassed for luxury. To celebrate his installation, he
entertained 600 guests at a dinner there. His list of courtiers
and court followers reads as a set-up of a seraglio of a Turkish
sultan or the Manchu court. Besides chamberlains, court valets,
chaplains, and personal physicians, he kept on his accounts a
gamekeeper, falconers, drummers and trumpeters, pages and
grooms, and an innumerable line of domestics. He also had a
personal ring-maker, a baker, a winder of clocks, and a rat
catcher. His dogs had their special baker of black bread, believed
to be a necessary nourishment for hunting dogs. As de Paule
grew older, his affection for court entourages grew greater and
the list longer.

The inquisitor had a field day criticizing the soft living and the
opulence at the magistral court. The feud worsened to such an
extent that, even with de Paule on his deathbed, the inquisitor
reported: 'The grand master is dying, but his irreverence is still

as alive as his sensuality, his selling of favours and twisting of justice to his own end, show his mastery of the art of duplicity.' Poor de Paule had certainly brought on his head the full ire of the inquisition, primarily as a result of Inquisitor Visconti's meddling in the knights' affairs. The bishop, too, claimed that de Paule showed complete indifference to censure, even when he publicly criticized the clergy by saying that 'briefs and citations are the priests' stock-in-trade'. De Paule's reign was never easy or free from quarrels.

At first, de Paule had to take some harsh measures which greatly offended the Italian knights who refused to obey his rulings. Some returned home and, aided and abetted by the inquisition, denounced de Paule to the pope as dishonest and corrupt. The grand master solicited the Christian kings to intervene and respectfully protested to Urban VIII, against such outright slander. But no help came. The whole Order was in a critical position, so much so that a general chapter was convened to determine the fate of the Order and what actions to take to stem its disintegration.

Urban VIII was forced to move. He appointed Inquisitor Serristori as president of the chapter general of the Order. There was an uproar and, to its credit, the Order, to a man, protested at this intrusion in the affairs of the Order. The pope immediately announced that he had 'suggested' the inquisitor as a neutral president and promptly explained that he was to have no vote and that he could not take part in the deliberations of the Order. Neither could he air his views about the matter in question. This compromise was accepted and the rebellious knights were prevailed upon to return to the Order. The inquisitor carried out his duty with dignity.

De Paule's troubles were also compounded by an invasion scare and the losses in naval battles, which were almost the first defeats in the Order's naval history. Urban VIII sent his

Grand Master Antoine de Paule
(Convent of St Ursula, Valletta)

engineer, Pietro Paolo Floriani, to examine and report on the defences of the island. Floriani reported that the open land on the landward side of Valletta was a great weakness in the defence of the city and had to be enclosed and fortified by walls stretching from the Grand Harbour to Marsamxett, thus denying the enemy any foothold adjacent to the city walls.

This suggestion proved to be controversial for many reasons. The knights complained that the report went against Laparelli's original advice that, by extending the defences, the entire position would be weakened. The other major problem was the lack of finances. A tax was imposed but, to keep the people quiet, it was decreed that this tax would be removed after three years. The work was begun but the grand master never lived to see it finished. It was finished by Perellos. The expected attack never took place but naval losses took their toll of the island's finances. On the rocky promontory at the mouth of the harbour, known as Gallows Hill, a tower was built to strengthen, together with St Elmo fort, the defence of entry to the harbour, named Orsi tower (also known by the Maltese as *Torri Teftef*) money for the construction of which was forthcoming from the Italian knight Francesco Orsi.

Towards the end of de Paule's reign, the Order, whose original duty was to act as custodian of the Holy Shrines of Jerusalem, had to witness the transfer of that responsibility of guardianship of the Holy Sepulchre from Roman Catholic administration to the Greek Schismatic rite.

During the last years of de Paule's magistracy, the inquisitor was Fabio Chigi who was to become Pope Alexander VII. He had been consecrated bishop by Bishop Balaguer on his arrival in Malta.

The greatly-maligned de Paule died on 10 June 1636 after a sudden illness, at the age of 84. He was buried in the chapel of

Fra Antoine de Paule's Mausoleum at St John's

(St John's Church, Valletta)

St Michael of the langue of Provence in St John's. His memory lives on among the thousands who have enjoyed his beautiful garden and magnificent palace which today is the official residence of the president of Malta.

Jean-Paul Lascaris-Castellar

1636-57

The gay court life was over. The credibility of the Order had suffered considerably at home and abroad. The Religion was riddled with internal fighting and accusations of loose living and corruption were laid against each and everyone. Discipline and honour were forgotten; yet those two prime virtues had to be recovered if the Order was to survive. In such a state of mind, the knights sought a man to lead them back to their former greatness. They found it in old Jean-Paul Lascaris-Castellar, an ascetic and lonely man, who was elected grand master at the age of 66.

Lascaris' grim features have remained as a Maltese expression of wryness and sourness in the expression *wiċċc laskri* (Lascaris' face), to the present day. At the same time, Lascaris could see that his young lusty bachelor knights needed a strong stern hand to keep them out of mischief in between their terms of service on the galleys. The good life at the langue's table, eating off silver plates and enjoying the best of foods imported from

Grand Master Jean-Paul Lascaris-Castellar

mainland Europe, was turning these once famous warriors into soft *gentil hommes*, more at home in the French court.

Lascaris rightly judged that they needed hard physical exercise and he therefore built a long, narrow enclosure for ball games, a *pallamaglio* (pall mall) now called *il-Mall*, just outside the main gate of Valletta. The Latin inscription on the entrance described the mall as a place where the knights, through play, gained strength in body and mind and steeled their hearts for warlike activities and kept their thoughts clean from vices, such as wine and women. Later, the first British commissioner, Sir Alexander Ball, converted the area into a garden of trees and flowers and opened it for the general public as recorded on a plaque at the entrance.

Although by this time a decline in the former glories was quite noticeable, yet the Order acquired, and held for a short period of two years, a sizeable colonial empire in the West Indies. In 1653, either to emulate the great European powers or to create a place where to dump troublesome knights on the pretext of colonization, Lascaris bought four West Indian islands, namely St Kitts, St Barthelemy, St Croix, and St Martin, from Louis XIV of France thus spreading the flag of St John to the New World. This venture of turning the knights of the Order into developers and managers of tropical estates was hardly a welcome experience for a hospitaller and Mediterranean sailor. Moreover, with the island population devastated by pestilence, the diminished workforce on the island was required for the building of fortifications. This empire-building was an eccentric move by an eccentric man and doomed to failure. In 1665 the knights gladly got rid of this useless encumbrance by selling the islands to the French West India Company. Luckily the Order made some profit out of this deal.

Lascaris' first thoughts were turned towards the defences of the island and its ability to withstand a siege. He immediately reinforced the walls of the city and increased its victualling capacity while things were peaceful and there seemed to be no threats from the east. Shrewd Lascaris knew that this was a lull before a storm and that all the Muslim world was preparing and waiting for the sultan to give the order to attack Malta. A programme of training the Maltese in the art of warfare was undertaken. Bormla was enclosed by walls, starting on Sta. Margerita heights, where the first stone was laid. These fortifications took a very long time to finish, and were only completed during Vilhena's rule. He also decided to strengthen the coastal defences. His great wish, he told the council, was to see the island completely surrounded by defended towers in order to secure all the shores. So he built a tower at Fomm-ir-Riħ and a stronger one at Ġnejna. On the south-west coast, he built two other towers, one at Wied iż-Żurrieq and another at Bubaqra on the outskirts of Żurrieq. These fortifications were paid for by the Maltese people and institutions.

In 1638, six Maltese galleys attacked 20 ships carrying goods from Tripoli to Sicily. At this time, Sicily was considered a hostile country because of its refusal to supply corn to the island. The knights captured the whole fleet and the Turkish chief, Ibrahim Rais, was taken prisoner on board the mighty galleon, the *Sultana*, after a bloody fight. This sea-battle is preserved for prosperity in a fresco in the Tapestry Chamber. What is most interesting about this engagement is that it would involve one of the most curious figures in the island's colourful history. One of the passengers on the Sultana was a young lady of high esteem, judging by her wardrobe and the splendour of her jewels. It was said that she was Zafire, one of the sultan's favourites who was travelling with her young son Osman, reputed to be Sultan Ibrahim's own son. Mother and son were taken to Malta where the mother died soon afterwards. The little boy proved to be a source of interest to the knights and was at first brought up as a 'pet' in the convent. He grew to be affectionate towards Lascaris who urged him to become a Christian. This the boy did with all his heart, and joined the Dominicans.

This affair immediately captured the imagination of the West: Ibrahim's son as a Christian was the biggest godsent for the Religion and Christendom, an event that could have great repercussions after Sultan Ibrahim's death. Alexander VII, who had been an inquisitor in Malta, called him to Rome and appointed him as messenger to bestow the pope's vestments to the Maltese churches. Padre Ottomano, as he now became called, was recalled to Rome where he stayed for a while, and was then sent on a tour of the royal courts of Europe, which was little short of a royal progress. In the court of Louis XIV, he, a rather retired shy priest, was feted by the elite of the French society.

Ibrahim had had enough of this eccentric behaviour of his Christian foes and he decided to avenge with one mighty hit the loss of a fleet and the insult of having Osman brought up in the Christian faith. The sultan ordered a massive attack although not on Malta this time. The assault was directed against Candia (Crete), the Venetian outpost that harboured the galleys of the Religion after their attack on the *Sultana*. Thus, in 1645 began the famous war of Candia which resulted in the capture of Crete by the Ottoman Empire in 1669.

And, at this point, the Christian potentates devised a grandiose but odd plan to throw confusion into the Turkish ranks: Osman was to proceed to Crete and proclaim himself as Ibrahim's son. He was to summon all Turkish subjects, both Muslims and Christians, to rally round him as the person combining the imperial Turkish blood and the Christian faith. If the person of Osman, the two great empires, the Byzantine and the Ottoman, were to combine into one great Christian State again. The plan was doomed to failure, for a start because of its impracticability.

Since Candia was not going well for the Venetians, the plot appeared ever more impossible. Padre Ottomano returned to Rome and, after a few years, he was sent back to Malta as vice-general of the Dominican Order. He resided at L-Isla where he died within a year of his return, a victim of the plague that was sweeping the island. He was 34 years old.

The great plague that swept the island decimated the population in and around the city and in the towns. It even reached Mdina. Lascaris thought of building a hospital on an island in Marsamxett (later known as Manoel Island) to stem the progress of the disease by quarantining the stricken. Prayers to St Roque, the protector from the plague, were answered just in time for the celebration of carnival, the three days of feasting and frolic before Lent.

It was then that another incident took place that was to have serious repercussions. Some young knights thought of playing a joke on the Jesuits to vent their dislike towards that Order of learned priests who never missed a chance of chastising their libertine lifestyle. Some young bloods dressed as Jesuits and paraded in the streets during carnival. The Jesuits protested to the ageing grand master and demanded that the culprits be punished severely.

Inquisitor Gori Pannellini, a very disagreeable man to both the Order and to Bishop Balaguer, seeing a good chance of intruding into the grand master's jurisdiction, demanded that the culprits be passed over to him for trial. This was naturally refused by the grand master who, however, promised that the most drastic action would be taken. Indeed Lascaris condemned the culprits to such a harsh punishment that most of the other knights revolted and demanded that the Jesuits should be expelled. A battle royal ensued. Finally, as a compromise suggested by the Jesuits, the culprits were let off with a light punishment with the understanding that the demand for the expulsion of the

Aerial view of Manoel Island

Jesuit Order would be allowed to die down, if not dropped altogether. In later years, the expulsion of the Jesuits would come up again and again. Lascaris donated an annuity to the Jesuit college to encourage the study of mathematics. He also issued a decree re-enforcing previous decrees for the establishment of a library from books of deceased knights. This laid the foundation for the library of the Order which was housed in a hall attached to the conventual church.

Lascaris immediately renewed active service for his young knights on board the fleet of the Religion. In 1644, the fleet attacked and captured a convoy of merchant ships on its way from Cephalonia to Cairo laden with rich merchandise. If the Order was jubilant, Sultan Ibrahim was not. He was outraged and once again vowed vengeance on the Order and the island that sheltered them. He immediately dispatched his ambassador to Lascaris with a declaration of war and began martial preparations. Lascaris did likewise, readying the fortifications and seeing to the victualling of the island.

However, Ibrahim did not launch any attack as he was advised to leave the fortified island alone and try for something easier and at the same time more hurtful to the enemy. So instead, the Turkish forces redoubled their attack on the strategic port of Candia that had served as an outpost first for the Genoese fleet and then for Venice and for the Order in their relentless attacks on Turkish shipping. The war of Candia dragged on to almost the end of the century.

With the pestilence and the threat of invasion over, the knights started to disagree among themselves about Lascaris' ascetic life at home and the liberal thoughts that were being imported from abroad, especially France. Intrigues abounded and conflicts made life very difficult for the grand master. He retreated even more within himself and would not communicate with anybody, except by growling at all around him. He called all those

Jean-Paul Lascaris-Castellar's Monument
(St John's Church, Valletta)

surrounding him, and even those overseas, vultures waiting for him to die. And on 14 August 1657, he met their wishes by passing away at the age of 77. Lascaris is buried in the chapel of St Michael in St John's.

Martin de Redin

1657-60

The passing of Grand Master Lascaris was met with a sigh of relief. The feuding and the intrigues that went on during the last years of his reign were blamed on the old man himself. The canvassing for his successor was fierce and prolonged. An Aragonese knight, the prior of St Navarre, canvassed well and long, and succeeded in being elected. Martin de Redin had served as a naval captain. He had built up a great reputation as commander of the Sicilian fleet and the king of Naples had even offered him the command of his fleet. De Redin also held the appointments of ambassador to the pope and to the king of Spain, the highest overseas appointments in the Order.

The feuding that went on prior to the death of Lascaris, coupled with the intrigues of electoral canvassing, gave the inquisitor grounds to criticize the Order. The withdrawal of the ageing Lascaris from public life and his brooding had made it quite easy for Inquisitor Oddi to encroach on the Order's jurisdiction. With the election of de Redin, Oddi shouted loud and clear that

Grand Master Martin de Redin

the process was rigged and invalid. He immediately left for Rome to appeal to Pope Alexander VII to declare the election invalid. The pope referred the case to the council of the Order, who advised him to confirm the election. Alexander ordered the inquisitor himself to convey the pope's approval to de Redin and, soon after, Oddi was recalled to Rome and nominated governor of Norcia.

With this trouble over, de Redin turned his attention to the completion of the coastal defences. He decreed that every headland had to be defended by a tower and he started building more watch towers around the shoreline and establishing an armoury in the larger villages. These armouries were intended to serve as arms and munitions stores for the surrounding

One of the watch towers built by de Redin

villages. In case of attack, the population could be armed quickly even if it was cut off from the cities.

An excellent example is Palazzo Armeria (built at Żurrieq during Pinto's reign), a fine spacious building set in six acres of orange and lemon trees, with its right corner dominated by a watch tower. From this tower, one could enjoy a clear view of Siggiewi and the hills of Rabat and Mdina to the north; the Grand Harbour to the east; the flat country of Ħal Far and beyond to Birżebbuġa to the south-east; and the islet of Filfla and the watchtower at Wied iż-Żurrieq to the south. This latter tower served its purpose again in the first days of the Second World War when it kept watch for enemy aircraft.

De Redin's three-year reign was packed with events and activity. He created work for the people by whom he was well respected. Perhaps the naming of savoury cheesecakes as *pastizzi tadderedin* has something to do with this.

The epitaph on de Redin's tomb in the chapel of Aragon in St John's says that he died on 6 February 1660. Some historians, however, date his death to 25 October 1659.

Annet de Clermont de Chettes-Gessan

1660

The knights, frightened of what would occur if another upheaval, like that had followed the election of de Redin, were to happen again, looked for a person who would be acceptable to most of the langues. Above all, they looked for someone who was neither controversial nor eccentric.

A kind and virtuous old Frenchman seemed to fit this picture. Annet de Clermont, balì of Lyon, was unanimously elected in February 1660. He had originally come to Malta as the emissary of Louis XIII of France to solicit help from Grand Master Wignacourt. France was then at war with the Huguenots and Louis needed the fleet of the Order. De Clermont did his job well and managed to persuade the fleet to join the French at Marseilles.

When he was elected, the old man was a battle-scarred and tired warrior. Soon the old battle wounds opened afresh and

Grand Master Annet de Clermont de Chettes-Gessan

Monument to Grand Master de Clermont

(St John's Church, Valletta)

started bleeding again and, within three months of his election, he bled to death. De Clermont passed away on 2 June 1660 and was buried in the chapel of St Sebastian of the langue of Auvergne, in St John's.

Rafael Cotoner

1660-63

The election of the old de Clermont and the rapid deterioration of his health stirred the former rivalries and hunger for power. Rather than risk all the controversies and outside interference as in the immediate past, canvassing for the magistracy was taken up early by the candidates, even while de Clermont lay on his deathbed. By the time he died, the corruption in electioneering was at its height. Plots and counter-plots were hatched by all and sundry. One candidate reunited nine suffrages to increase his voting powers while others did likewise until the whole thing became so scandalous that it was impossible to hold the election. The council was obliged to appoint a commissioner to choose a successor to de Clermont.

The choice fell on Rafael Cotoner, balì of Majorca. A few knights protested and argued the validity of the election or, rather, appointment. However, the man proved to be the best choice in the long run and Rafael Cotoner was destined to write another glorious chapter in the history of the Order and of Malta. In a

Grand Master Rafael Cotoner

Mattia Preti, "St John baptising Christ" (above) and
"God the Eternal bestowing His Blessing" – the vault, St John's

(St John's Church, Valletta)

Mattia Preti, "Priests and Levites question St John" (above) and
"The Beheading of St John the Baptist"

(St John's Church, Valletta)

Monument to Grand Master Rafael Cotoner

(St John's Church, Valletta)

very short time, his devotion, virtue, and zeal for work at home
and abroad made him not only acceptable but a favourite with
his knights, both young and old. He kept the young ones occupied
fighting the Turks, and brought back the glories of old to the
old knights. For the islanders, he created work and encouraged
commerce. One of his great works was the enlargement of the
great ward of the Sacred Infirmary to over 500 feet and opened
a school of anatomy. By now the Sacred Infirmary was
considered to be the most famous public hospital in Europe to
which rich and poor flocked, a place where all were treated
with the same care and ate from silver plates. To glorify St
John's, together with his brother Nicolas who was to succeed
him to the office, he embellished the church with great paintings
which still hold visitors in awe at the whole splendour. The
painting of the vault was carried out by the famous Calabrian
painter Mattia Preti

This was a restless period in the Mediterranean. In the east,
the Turks had been trying to wrest Candia from the Venetians,
while in the west the corsairs of Tripoli were creating great
trouble causing major losses to Christian trading ships. The
grand master kept his young officers fully engaged in the
fighting in Candia until it was lost to the Turks. During the
struggle, the knights and soldiers of the Order won so much
honour that Venice decided to bestow on the Order the highest
honour of all: the knights were given the right to wear their
weapons on Venetian soil, a right not even given to Venetians.

In 1663, the plague struck again, this time ravaging Valletta.
Cotoner fell sick. On his death bed, surrounded by all the
dignitaries sincerely praying that such a good administrator
and benefactor be spared, he commended his brother Nicolas
as his successor.

Cotoner died on 20 October 1663, aged 63, and was buried in
the chapel of Aragon in his beloved St John's.

Nicolas Cotoner

1663-80

Rafael Cotoner was so beloved by everyone that no one could ignore his last wish. And so Nicolas succeeded him as grand master, the lord prince of the island.

It had always been expected that great things would flow from the Cotoners. Nicolas too did not disappoint anyone, nor disgrace his brother. On the contrary, he outshone him. A wise and valiant leader, he had fought well and hard in the war of Candia which dragged on for 22 long years with many ups and downs.

For centuries, Candia had lain in the hands of the Venetians. Nicolas followed his brother's policy of fighting the enemy as far away from home shores as possible. He kept on supplying ships, men, and armaments and did all he could to help rebuff the Muslim assaults. Grand Vizier Ahmed, impatient with the solid stand of the Christian princes, decided to lead a last attack himself and personally capture the port and fortified citadel.

Grand Master Nicolas Cotoner

This he accomplished in 1669. But, before this, the Turkish fleet had suffered a great defeat at the hands of the combined fleets of Venice and the Order. This greatly annoyed the Turkish commander who immediately started to plot for the total annihilation of the Order's fleet. Once he defeated the Venetians, he entered into a treaty of unilateral peace with Venice and started to rebuild his fleet.

Cotoner was aghast, since Venice, for whom the Order had provided so much help and fought so long and so hard, was now aligning itself with its perpetual enemy. Concerned about the safety of the island, Cotoner started to look at the strength of the island's fortifications. At the mouth of the harbour opposite St Elmo, Fort Ricasoli rose in the defence of the harbour opening and, to the right of Ricasoli, Fort St Roque was built to defend the hinterland behind the three cities and the land approach to Fort St Angelo. To improve the defences further, he commis-sioned the construction of the Cottonera lines. This great defensive work is commemorated by the magnificent gate at Żabbar. This archway, adorned with the bust of this great grand master, has an inscription extolling his grace and kindness to all, his greatness in peace and war, and his fame through his kingdom and throughout the world. It bears the date 1675.

At the same time the Order's fleet kept its pressure on Muslim ships that were harassing Christian trade. Its prowess drew the attention of Charles II of England who was being greatly harassed by his subjects to do something to defend English merchant shipping in the Mediterranean. In 1647 Charles dispatched a squadron under Admiral Sir John Narborough with express orders to clear the seas from corsairs operating off Tripoli.

Writing to the grand master, Charles commended the admiral and his squadron to the goodwill of the 'most eminent Prince

The magnificent gate at Żabbar

and Lord Nicolas Cotoner, grand master of the Order of Malta, our Cousin, and very dear friend' and he asked that the admiral and his ships be treated in the Order's territory as allies and friends and to be allowed to buy needs and provisions at a fair price.

The expected attack on Malta never happened but instead the Turks attacked Italian shores. The island, however, did not escape another outbreak of the plague which was so severe that another building, an isolation hospital, was hastily erected on the islet in Marsamxett harbour that later became known as Manoel Island. A member of the English squadron describes it so: 'The Lazzaretto (a place on purpose for such as are sick of the plague or other pestilential diseases, which in regard of the heat of that country do often range there) lies close under their outermost wall, and is extremely neatly kept and provided for.'

The outbreak hit almost every household, rich and poor; the people, young and old, died by the thousands. Prayers were offered in every church and the·grand master vowed to rebuild the old chapel at Sarria into a beautiful church in honour of the Immaculate Virgin Mary in gratitude for Her intercession. The Order's strength in fighting men was greatly reduced and this caused Cotoner much anxiety and distress. The Turkish enemy, noticing this weakness, immediately set upon the Order's fleet, then engaged in protecting the Italian shores. The fleet of the Order was beaten and had to retreat to its home port to avoid complete annihilation.

Most of Nicolas' reign was a glorious period of greatness and prosperity. Cotoner laid down humane laws, strove for better health and hygiene, and provided justice for the weak. He achieved greatness in art and architecture, both in St John's; and in the adornment of magnificent buildings. Unfortunately towards the end of his reign, Nicolas saw his beloved land and

Sarria Church, Floriana

Nicolas Cotoner's monument

(St John's Church, Valletta)

subjects devastated with yet another outbreak of the plague, to be followed by a great famine in 1659. Broken-hearted, he fell ill and died on 29 April 1680, aged 73. To commemorate the magnificence of such a truly great prince, a great mausoleum was erected in the chapel of Aragon in St John's.

Gregorio Caraffa

1680-90

Long before the death of Nicolas Cotoner, the old rivalries started to re-emerge owing to the lack of any worthy successor. The battle was on, the French langues lining up their candidate Adrien Wignacourt, while the Italian-Spanish faction had their leader in the Aragonese Gregorio Caraffa. It was Caraffa, prior of Rocella and resident in Naples, who was elected on 2 May 1680. The choice was again a wise one, for Caraffa proved himself truly worthy of the Cotoners. His reign was mostly full of glory and grandeur, interspersed with deeds of knightly valour and marked with splendid works of art all around the island.

On his accession, Caraffa turned his attention to rebuilding his fighting fleet. Soon, the flag of the Religion was again sweeping the Mediterranean and chasing the Barbary corsairs into their lairs at a time when the Muslim empire seemed to be at its zenith, harassing the shores of Italy at will and commanding the Mediterranean, both east and west, and also the Adriatic sea.

Grand Master Gregorio Caraffa

The miraculous icon of Our Lady of Carafa,
named after its doner, Gregorio Caraffa

(St John's Church, Valletta)

The ships of the Order mercilessly attacked Muslim ships and Turkish outposts, plundering as they went. The treasury of the Order bulged with money and Caraffa made good use of it to give the people security by extending fortifications and building hospitals. He built and adorned churches across the island and created work for all, greatly enlarging the armed services on land and sea.

The admiration of Pope Innocent XI for the knights was so great that he expressed his gratitude to the grand master and the Order in a Brief, praising them for their valour in the liberation of the shores of Italy from the barbarians. The pope also directed Bishop Cocco Palmeri to co-operate with the grand master. Thus, for the very first time, one could say that the Order and Church enjoyed a happy co-existence to the detriment of the inquisition. Inquisitor Caracciolo clashed with both the new bishop and the knights, but his natural meekness in the face of poverty made him dear to the hearts of the common man and many a tear was shed on his departure in May 1668.

Caraffa had a long reign, but when the first reversal of fortune hit, he could not withstand failure and disappointment. In 1689 the ships of the Religion suffered a severe defeat at Negroponte. Caraffa's disappointment at such a humiliation caused his death. He fell ill and died on 21 July 1690, aged 76.

Though a lifelong believer in the greatness of the Order in war and in peace, Caraffa retained his humility unto death. During his lifetime, he built his own tomb and wrote his epitaph: 'Let this be my resting place and not a monument.'

Adrien de Wignacourt

1690-97

This time, Wignacourt's backers made sure that their contender would not be passed over again. In spite of the old election rivalries that again raised their head, the French side held the cards, and Adrien de Wignacourt was elected.

Wignacourt lost no time in proving himself another worthy claimant to the princely office. Within a short time he earned a high reputation for his piety and generosity. The wars against the infidel had been long and bloody and had left many a family bereft of its breadwinner. Moreover, the pestilence had also left many 'one-parent' families. Out of his generosity, Wignacourt extended help to the many orphans about and encouraged his knights to act as benefactors to these orphans and widows of fallen seamen and soldiers.

In Wignacourt's time, in 1693, a great earthquake hit the island. The catastrophe hit both Sicily and Malta where damage was considerable and many families lost all their belongings. So

185

Grand Master Adrien de Wignacourt

The chapel of France at St John's which houses
Adrien de Wignacourt's mausoleum

(St John's Church, Valletta)

severe were the tremors that the whole population was terrified, and a rumour spread like wildfire that the earthquake was a sign from heaven, a punishment from God. People flocked to churches and prayed and made reparations by way of fasting and sacrifices. They held processions in the streets and dedicated whole towns and villages to patron saints. The Church still reminds the Maltese population of this catastrophe every year by the singing of the *Te Deum* in all churches.

Immediately after the tremors, the good grand master toured the island, visiting the bereaved families, giving his own money to the needy, and putting men to work immediately to repair the damage. Wherever he went, the crowd gathered around him and kissed his hand in reverence. Evidence of his work of restoration may be still seen on the many buildings adorned with his coat-of-arms.

As Wignacourt got older, he became weaker. Saddened with the sufferings of his poor people, he passed away on 4 February 1697, venerated by all. He was buried under a magnificent mausoleum in the chapel of France at St John's. He was 79.

Ramon Perellos y Rocaful

1697-1720

The Order lost no time in selecting a successor to the revered Wignacourt. Within three days, an upright man from Aragon, Ramon Perellos y Rocaful, balì of Negroponte, was elected.

Perellos took advantage of the newly-built fleet that had by now re-established itself as a formidable adversary to the Turkish counterpart. The fights and the chases between the Maltese and Turkish fleets were at their peak. In one of their most notable successes the Maltese ships captured a fabulous prize, the *El-Binghan*, the pride of the Turkish fleet, together with several other smaller ships, all laden with precious goods. The Turks gave chase right to the shores of the island, literally taking command of the Gozo straits.

Perellos could not ignore this direct threat to the island. The man of the hour was Balì Zondadari who advised attacking the Turkish ships plying along the Sicilian coast. Zondadari was a forceful man, a man accustomed to being listened to, and a

Grand Master Ramon Perellos y Rocaful

man with the right connections at the Vatican, being a nephew of Alexander VII and a brother to a cardinal. His naval strategy saved Malta from immediate attack. Later he again proved to be a saviour to both the Order and the Maltese in getting the inquisition subdued. An incident in the streets of Valletta between the two archenemies, the grand master and the inquisitor, was perhaps the last straw.

It was the prerogative for the grand master's coach to take precedence on the streets over any other coach, including that of the inquisitor. Should the inquisitor in his coach meet the grand master on foot, the inquisitor was expected to alight, bow to him, pay a compliment, and proceed. And if the grand master was riding and the inquisitor walking, the inquisitor was expected to bow profoundly to the grand master without accosting the coach. One day the coaches met in a rather narrow street in Valletta and, by intention or by accident, the inquisitor's coach blocked the street, forcing the grand master's coach to halt and give way. This incident caused a furore and was seen as a flagrant breach of protocol and an insult to the magistracy.

The next day, the inquisitor, trying to patch things up, followed the grand master to the Sacred Infirmary, but made the unpardonable mistake of entering the infirmary armed. Even the grand master, as was the custom, had left his baton at the door. The grand master, sensing trouble both at home and at the Vatican, immediately appealed to the pope to recall the inquisitor. The inquisitor was replaced.

The fight for the supremacy of the Mediterranean continued unabated. Battles were fought along the shores of Africa and Sicily. The fleet of the Religion, now widely known as the Maltese naval force, suffered a great defeat at the battle of Oran. The fall of Oran so shocked the grand master that he had a stroke and was administered the last sacraments but he survived to carry on the fight. The attacks on Gozo increased in number and ferocity, yet the Turks were not confident enough to mount a direct attack on Malta. The grand master built another three new fighting ships out of his own money in order to strengthen the naval force. The ships celebrated their maiden voyage by capturing a heavily-laden Turkish merchant ship and chasing away the two galleys protecting it.

The nations of northern Europe were also starting to make moves for supremacy in the Mediterranean. Peter the Great of Russia sent his envoy to Perellos to suggest an alliance against the Turks. The grand master, sensing it as a ruse for Russia to obtain a foothold in the Mediterranean, diplomatically refused the offer, on the excuse that there were requests from the pope to stop harassing the Turkish fleet without provocation. The English fleet was also constantly sailing in and out of Valletta engaged in protecting fellow merchant shipping and in clearing the sea lanes from Barbary corsairs. To keep the Protestants at a distance from the Catholic islanders, the English ships were given a berth in 'English Creek', now known as Rinella Creek, between Kalkara Creek and Ricasoli Point. The French fully understood the dependency of the island on the money flowing into the treasury from the French commendaries and were quite pleased seeing the magistracy keeping other potentates at bay. After all, French kings could not interfere too much in the affairs of the island without offending Spain, Venice, and, most of all, the Vatican. Spain and the kingdom of the Two Sicilies (Sicily and Naples) were satisfied with the situation as the island was still morally and nominally theirs and their might was fast diminishing.

Perellos, whose previous stroke had left him infirm, fell ill in June 1719 and, on 10 January 1720, passed away, a tired man, at the age of 83. Perellos is buried in the chapel of Aragon in St John's.

Perellos' other major monuments were the sets of magnificent

Two of the fifteen tapestries at St John's Museum –
"The Raising of the Cross" (above) and "The Resurrection"
(St John's Church, Valletta)

"The Ostriches", one of the French tapestries
at the Magistral Palace, Valletta

(The Palace, Valletta)

Another French tapestry at the Palace, "The King Borne"

Porte des Bombes

tapestries he donated to St John's and to the Magistral Palace. The former set of fifteen tapestries can today be admired in the museum of St John's. The set in the council chamber in the Magistral Palace were made in France in 1713. The grand master also built a very imposing entry gate to Valletta through the fortified walls of Floriana, called Porte des Bombes. Modern governments have reduced this once imposing structure into a mere shadow of its former grandeur in order to accommodate traffic. Always alert over the defence of the island, he strengthened, amongst other sites, the fort of St Elmo by extending the bastions around it.

Marc'Antonio Zondadari

1720-22

Nephew of Pope Alexander VII, Marc'Antonio Zondadari was born in Siena of an ancient Italian aristocratic house. He served his apprenticeship on board the galleys of the Religion in Naples. From his early days, he showed an intrepid character and an unshakeable determination to master his profession as a naval officer. Grand Master Caraffa appointed him commander to three fleets and by 1707 he became grand esquire, counsellor, and confidant to Perellos. His naval ability and valuable words of advice earned him the top naval appointment as admiral of the fleet.

Never, it is recorded, did he take advantage of his parentage or abuse his family lineage for personal gain, but rather his virtues prompted him to be of service, thus endearing himself to his fellow knights and to the ordinary man.

Zondadari's very first act on his election was, against some opposition, to admit to the Maltese that his predecessors had

Grand Master Marc'Antonio Zondadari

The *Banca Giuratale*, Merchants Street, Valletta

completely eroded the people's privileges. On presenting himself
at the gates of Mdina to receive the keys of the city from the
jurats, he refused to take the oath to preserve the rights and
privileges of the *Università* since, he declared, 'there were no
more privileges left to uphold', and that he was not going to
swear to God an empty and useless oath. There was great
jubilation and festivities in his honour in the towns and villages
around the island. He renamed Bormla 'Cospicua' acknowledging
the strong fortifications surrounding it. To acknowledge his
recognition of the rights of the Maltese, he built the *Banca
Giuratale*, the administrative building of the *Università* (the
seat of public administration), where the *Hakem*, the chief
magistrate, and the four jurats sat.

The Order's naval force, as if to celebrate his election, captured
and escorted into harbour two large Muslim ships headed by
the Algerian flagship. Victory followed victory until the sea lanes
were cleared and the Maltese navy became mistress of the
central Mediterranean, so much so that Muslim ships would
chose to remain in port if Maltese ships were reported nearby.

Within a year of his election, Zondadari fell ill. After six full
months of suffering, he passed away on 6 June 1722, aged 64.
Mourned by all, he was buried by the main entrance of St John's.
His heart is, however, buried in Siena, the ancestral home of
his illustrious family.

Anton Manoel de Vilhena

1722-36

Anton Manoel de Vilhena was born a prince, lived as a prince, and died as a prince. His princely ways and air, his magnificence, and his pageantry endeared him to his subjects. The people loved a show and he gave them plenty of royal splendour and princely benevolence. Since his boyhood, Manoel had shown a flair for swashbuckling. Joining the Order while still a young lad, his promotions had followed in rapid succession. Appointed captain at the age of 18, he was wounded several times and earned high praise and decorations. The next few years saw his promotion first to major, then to colonel.

At the age of 33, Manoel became the youngest grand cross of grace in the history of the Order. Two years later, he became grand chancellor. In 1703 he was appointed balì of Acre.

During the latter years of Perellos' reign, Manoel's name had become a legend and he was hero-worshipped by the young members of the Order. On the death of good old Perellos, he

Grand Master Anton Manoel de Vilhena

staked his claim to the magistracy backed by the Spanish and Portuguese knights but lost to Zondadari because of the Italian's special qualities, lineage, and the special place he held within the Order, especially in the eyes of Perellos.

Still Zondadari's successor could be none other than Anton Manoel de Vilhena. He was indeed elected on 19 July 1722, a month after Zondadari's death.

This militant Order of Hospitallers that had established itself on a rocky island-shelter to wage perpetual war with the enemy was now in the eighteenth century when the arts of peace were asserting themselves over the arts of war. Vilhena immediately set himself to build palaces and beautiful things. He soon acquired the fame of a great builder.

But, before that name was on the lips of every inhabitant, an incident took place that made his name resound all over the Christian world in praise and all through the Saracen lands in hatred. Some time after his election, a Turkish slave called Ali escaped from the island. He informed the grand vizier in Turkey that the Turkish slaves on Malta outnumbered the inhabitants and, what was more important, that they were not seriously supervised, security being loose. The informer persuaded the vizier that an uprising was easy to arrange and the seizing of the island from inside was a certainty.

By sheer luck and because the slaves were in general humanely treated, the plot was reported early to the grand master. Vilhena immediately went into action and isolated all Turkish slaves on Manoel island without too much ill-treatment. When Admiral Abdi lead his fleet to the attack, the revolt having failed to take place, he had to beat a hasty retreat. To save his humiliation, before he set sail, Abdi sent an ultimatum to the grand master demanding, in the name of his mighty sultan, the immediate release of all Turkish slaves on the island, failing which he

would personally order all the might of the Ottoman world to
take revenge by killing all Christians, slaves or otherwise, in
their territory. Vilhena stood firm and the slaves were not
released. The Turkish fleet sailed away but later returned to
bombard the city. The attack was repulsed and the Maltese
ships hit back. In the ensuing battle, the Turkish admiral was
captured on board the *Kali-Muhamet*.

The whole Christian world went jubilant. Benedict XIII
presented Vilhena with the stock and pilier. The stock was a
casque of purple velvet adorned with the symbolic dove of peace,
while the pilier was a bare sword with a lavishly-adorned
pommel. This was a supreme papal distinction, bestowed on
very few emperors, such as Philip II of Spain.

Peace being assured for the island, Vilhena became the great
builder and protector of the arts. The theatre prospered; in 1731
he built a gem of a theatre in Valletta which, to this day, after
a chequered life, still delights patrons. Originally called the
Public Theatre, the name was changed to Manoel Theatre when
the opera house was built near City Gate. It opened its doors on
19 January 1732 'for the honest recreation of the people' with
the presentation of the opera *Merope*. One of the oldest theatres
in Europe still in regular use, it has an ordinary-looking exterior
but the interior, planned after the Palermo theatre, and is
delightfully decorated.

Palaces were adorned and life became very pleasant in the
city. Just inside the gates of Mdina, opposite the old beacon
tower which used to warn the people of enemy landings,
Manoel built a palace right on the ramparts of the ancient
city, a city he loved and of which he can be deemed a second
founder. He presented this palace, now called Vilhena Palace,
to the *Università*, perhaps as reparation for his predecessors'
attitude of whittling away the rights they all had sworn to
preserve on their elevation to the magistracy. Called the

Main gate, Mdina, clearly showing Vilhena's coat-of-arms

Vilhena Palace, Mdina

Magistral Palace, it served as the courts of justice for the *Università*.

Manoel did not forget the common man by whom he was truly loved. He built the residential suburb of Floriana for the benefit and well-being of his subjects, behind the well-defended walls planned by the engineer Pietro Floriani. In St Anne Square, he raised a fountain dominated by a statue of a lion, the symbol of Manoel and of his beloved suburb. He also named the suburb after him, 'Vilhena', and honoured it with his coat-of-arms. However, the people chose to stick the former name of Floriana and to incorporate Vilhena's lion as part of the coat-of-arms of the suburb.

Manoel also built a hospital for incurables and a refuge for poor women and homeless single mothers. In his princely magnificence, he forgot no one. And when it came to his personal comfort, perhaps there is no better example of his domestic tastes than his country house at Santa Venera. This Baroque villa, *Dar l-Ljuni* (House of the Lions) as it is known, looks plain and unassuming, the only external adornments being the four lions of the grand master's coat-of-arms, from which the villa takes its name. Inside there is an elaborate eighteenth-century Mediterranean garden, about eight acres in area divided into three parts, each of which enclosed by architecturally-adorned stone walls. Manoel's coat-of-arms of rampant lions and winged sword adorns the ornamental arches through which one gazes at trees of oranges and mandarins, laden with blossoms and golden fruit, and at the graceful fountain in the top garden. During the 1939-45 war it served as the courts of law when these were bombed out at Valletta and, later, as a primary school.

Inside the city gate, Manoel helped the Conventual Friars to accomplish their great and long-standing wish to rebuild their church, known as *San Frangisk ta' Putirjal* (St Francis at the

Fort Manoel

Monument to Anton Manoel de Vilhena
(St John's Church, Valletta)

Royal Gate, that is, the main gate of Valletta), the earlier one attached to the convent, being by then too small.

In 1727 Manoel accepted the oft-repeated request of the Jesuit College for the institution of an academy with the full powers of conferring degrees in philosophy and theology, in short, giving the college the title and the academic authority of a university.

To secure the inner waters of Marsamxett and Valletta's northern flank, Manoel commissioned the French engineers Mondion to design a fortress on Lazaretto islet (later renamed Manoel Island) and Tignè to build and fortify it with armaments respectively.

The much-beloved Manoel reigned for fourteen years, a reign marked with progress and prosperity, of greatness in the arts.

Anton Manoel de Vilhena died, aged 73, on 12 December 1736. Never did a nation mourn so deeply the loss of its *sultan* (ruler). He was buried in the chapel of Castille and Portugal in St John's.

Ramon Despuig

1736-41

A descendant of an illustrious Spanish house, Ramon Despuig, balì of Majorca, was elected grand master on 16 December 1736. He was a born administrator, his ability as such being undisputed. He had already been called upon three times to perform the duty of acting grand master.

Despuig's predecessors had done a great job of harassing Muslim shipping along the western shores of Africa and the Sicilian coast, and the Maltese navy had managed to secure their island from the constant marauding of the Muslim corsairs. However, the eastern seaboard of the Mediterranean was controlled by the Turkish navy which was causing havoc to Venetian shipping, despite heavy losses.

On his accession Despuig immediately exchanged the pen for the sword. He devoted all his efforts and those of the country to get rid of the infestation of the eastern seas by hostile Muslim fighting galleys and pirate vessels.

Grand Master Ramon Despuig

Fort Tignè

Despuig decreed that neither he nor any of his men would rest until the enemy was destroyed and Christian shipping was free to trade the high seas without fear of attack and the consequent ending of trade in Christians on the slave market. Despuig's first priority of his magistracy, as he saw it, was to end all Turkish influence in the Mediterranean and he would not rest until the seas were cleared. Only then did he lay down his sword and rest. A long period of peace followed which stretched to the reign of his successor. With his preoccupation of waging war, Despuig had no time for the magistracy although he insisted that the assembly had to keep pace in the administration of the affairs of the nation. In order to keep them fired with enthusiasm, he decided to get famous speakers to give an annual oration to the assembly. This annual address by famous orators became an institution.

But Despuig did not overlook the defences of the island. He instructed the French engineer Tignè to start on the construction of a fort designed earlier on the tongue of land jutting out at the mouth of Marsamxett, known as Dragut Point. This fort, which was named after the same engineer, was completed during the rule of Rohan.

Despuig passed away on 15 January 1741 and was buried in the chapel of Aragon in St John's. In 1740 he had donated a marble top for the high altar of the conventual church.

Emmanuel Pinto

1741-73

Three days after the death of Despuig, the Portuguese Emmanuel Pinto de Fonseca was elected grand master.

Pinto's predecessors had been taking on themselves lavish and princely attributes which were reflected in the splendour of their court. Pinto's reign marks a further advance to regal status. The magnificence of his reign is the supreme example of an absolute monarch ruling over Malta. In his later portraits, Pinto achieves the ultimate and is shown wearing a closed crown, with gold and ermine completely replacing the black magistral bonnet. The crucifix and the book of devotions are replaced by the stock and pilier.

The magnificent Pinto enjoyed the first years of his reign in peace. A life of lavish entertainment at the court was marred only by the final break with the Jesuits, ending in their expulsion in 1769. Pinto established the first university on the foundations of the suppressed Jesuits' college in Valletta, which soon became

215

Grand Master Emmanuel Pinto

a great centre of learning, having replaced the Jesuit scholars by the best of Italian professors and lecturers. Commerce enjoyed the greatest confidence both on land and sea. Apart from moments of tension with the traditional enemy, maritime trading was brisk both in the east and west Mediterranean even to the shores of Turkish dependencies, taking advantage of the trading friendship between France and the Ottoman empire at the time. Maltese cotton found a ready market in France, where Maltese were considered as citizens, and along the Mediterranean shores of Spain.

In 1748 an extremely dangerous conspiracy was unmasked. At that time, the Turkish prisoners held in Malta were treated very humanely. One such prisoner was none other than the illustrious Mustapha Pasha of Rhodes. He had been well-received by his captors and treated as a high ranking prisoner-of-war. Whether the capture of the pasha was engineered by the Turks in order to infiltrate the fortress island with a secret agent will never be known. The fact remains that Mustapha secretly started plotting Pinto's assassination.

He secured the services of two Greeks and two Jews to carry out the execution. The plan was to kill the grand master, poison the water supply, and, in the confusion, release all Turkish prisoners. Pinto's valet, a Muslim slave, was enlisted to stab his master. Three times he tried, he confessed later, and three times he could not bear to do it. He could not bring himself to hurt his benefactor, he declared. The next attempt was at poisoning the grand master's food. This again failed when the Muslim attendant hesitated and abandoned the attempt. Rumours started to spread and the two Jews turned informers and denounced the whole plot. Mustapha was indicted and he eventually confessed, placing the blame on his sovereign Mehmed V and naming 40 others as main conspirators who were all summarily hanged. Pinto was horrified at this barbarous treatment and decreed that

Favray: Portrait of Grand Master Emmanuel Pinto

(St John's Museum)

Monument to Grand Master Emmanuel Pinto

(St John's Church, Valletta)

henceforth the hanging of slaves as mere punishment was to be abolished.

It was the offer to assume sovereignty over Corsica that made Pinto inclined to bestow on himself the dignity of a sovereign. The offer was not taken up owing to the intervention of the duke of Choisel who was afraid that such an act would not be looked upon favourably by the king of France who then proceeded to take over the island himself. However, from then on, Pinto started using a closed crown, a symbol of sovereignty, yet he would not allow himself to be addressed as 'Majesty' although he would not tolerate being addressed by his previous title of 'Eminence'. His defence was that since one of his predecessors, namely Alof de Wignacourt in 1609, had been regaled with the title of 'Prince of the Holy Roman Empire' he and his successors were entitled to be addressed as 'Serene Highness'. He settled for the compromise 'Eminent Highness'.

Pinto lived to the ripe old age of 92, surrounding himself with beautiful works of art and music. He died on 25 January 1773 and was buried in the chapel of Castille and Portugal in St John's.

Perhaps an even greater mausoleum to his greatness is the Auberge de Castille, the most beautiful of all the auberges both from the inside and the outside. Originally built by the Maltese architect Gerolamo Cassar in 1574, the building was reconstructed by Pinto and transformed into a palace fit for a sovereign. It now houses the office of the prime minister of Malta.

Pinto also paid attention to the fortifications by strengthening the ones in disrepair and building new ones, including Pinto battery with 13 gun emplacements; Bengħajsa Tower, which was armed with ten guns; and batteries and redoubts around Birżebbuġa Bay and Spinola Tower armed with two guns.

Francesco Ximenes

1773-75

On 28 January 1773 the Spaniard Francesco Ximenes, grand prior of Navarre, was elected grand master.

If there was anything of note about Ximenes, it was his ability to make enemies. He was the complete antithesis of his beloved predecessor. His past had nothing worthy to show which could earn him the magistracy. As seneschal to Pinto, he had administered the Order and the land while Pinto reigned over his knights and the people. Ximenes was of a hard and cynical nature, very severe and ascetic. He hit hard those who erred and those who, in his eyes, lived luxuriously and abused the administration. To those who served him, he returned loyalty with haughtiness and disdain. In short, he made himself repugnant to all around him and lost all the affection that previous grand masters had generated amongst the Maltese towards their *sultan*.

It is said that during Ximenes' period as senechal, Pinto

Grand Master Francesco Ximenes

borrowed large sums of money from a Marsa church dedicated to the souls in Purgatory to build large stores at Marsa which he rented to merchants. The rents were directed to the Order's treasury. The story goes that when the Church asked for the return of the money borrowed, or at least for interest on that money, the senechal replied that when his master, the grand master, passed on and went to purgatory, he would fix things up with them himself.

The new university went into heavy debt because the money from the rent of the stores, built by other previous grand masters, and from the property of the expelled Jesuits was not sufficient to pay its heavy expenses. To reduce expenditure, the grand master replaced most of the teaching staff with local lecturers at lower pay and imposed a new tax on bread. This infuriated the people and to some it was the last straw. Events happened quickly and nearly cost Ximenes the crown, the island, and the Order. With Europe in ferment and rebellious moods in France, similar thoughts drifted to Malta. A faction of priests and nobles, together with a few knights, formed the nucleus of a rebellion against the Order. The aim was to push the Order out and install a popular government.

As head of the revolt, which came to be known as 'The Rising of the Priests', was appointed a simple and credulous priest, Don Gaetano Mannarino. The conspirators waited for the fleet of the Order to be out at sea. At dead of night, they attacked St Elmo which was to serve two purposes: one, to ensure the sealing of the harbour against the return of the fleet, and two, as the headquarters of the uprising. Once this was achieved, the Maltese population in and around the city were to rise, join in with the confederates, attack the palace, and seize the grand master. St Elmo was captured. Two hundred prisoners were taken and the Maltese flag was hoisted. But, on the march to the palace, 'the man in the street' failed to join in. The grand master, awakened, immediately summoned the help of a handful of knights and, with the element of surprise on his side, soon crushed the revolt.

Mannarino's co-plotters paid the ultimate penalty on the main palace square. He himself was imprisoned for life and only released later by the French in June 1798.

Ximenes was terribly shocked, to the extent that he died within two months. He is remembered for the extension of the Customs House and the Castello at Rabat, Gozo. Right up to his death, he insisted that the heads of the conspirators be kept displayed stuck on a lance on the bastions as a grim warning to all would-be revolutionaries.

Ximenes was not so heavy-handed with the bishop when the latter furiously opposed his edict against the hunting of rabbits. The grand master had decided to increase the food supply of the island by restocking it with game and had issued an edict forbidding game hunting for a certain period. The bishop complained loudly that famine would result as the increasing rabbit population would ruin the crops. The grand master, sensing the real reason for the episcopal opposition, i.e. that the Curia may have to increase the daily stipend of the clergy because of lack of free food from the hunting grounds, relented. To oblige the bishop, he exempted episcopal lands, until he found out that the bishop interpreted the concession as a right to kill rabbits not only for himself, but also for his canons and all the other clergy and all those who came under the jurisdiction and administration of the Curia.

Ximenes died on 11 November 1775. He was buried in St John's in the most obscure place of the crypt, forgotten by everyone.

Emmanuel de Rohan

1775-97

The short and troubled reign of Ximenes was followed by the long and most humane reign of Emmanuel de Rohan. Born while his noble father was in hiding in Spain, he had been baptized Fran ois-Marie de Neges Emmanuel. He was nominated knight of justice and soon showed great promise for the future. On arriving in Malta, he was appointed balì and was later handed command of the Order's fleet.

Throughout his reign, Rohan proved a kind ruler. Soon after his election, he ordered the removal from the bastions of the heads of the conspirators of the uprising against his predecessor. He was a man with an open and inquiring mind, enjoying people and social life; for the first time, he allowed ladies to attend court receptions.

Without doubt, Rohan's court was influenced by events in the French court where the very survival of its king and queen was being menaced. The theories of the French Revolution were

Grand Master Emmanuel de Rohan

penetrating into the auberges of the Order and already some of the young knights were discussing quite openly the equality of men, which was in dire contrast to the Order's recruiting principles of perpetuating the aristocratic line of society.

On Rohan's election, the French knights went wild and great festivities were held for there had been no French grand master since 1697.

One of his first thoughts, among a string of reforms, was to combine the two institutes for the poor and the oppressed, the *Monte di Redenzione* and the *Monte di Pietà*, set up some 200 years earlier by Grand Master Garzes.

In the short space of three years, Rohan carried out several important reforms that his predecessors had failed to do. One of his great achievements was the completion of a code which had originally been conceived by Manoel in 1723. The code, called 'Code Rohan', together with the Justinian Code, forms the basis of the common law of Malta; it is a well-coded (written) law to protect all, rich or poor. It was the first to be drawn up completely compatible with the character of the Maltese people and was published in 1782. In the upheaval of a changing world, the code contained a great number of reforms which were mostly received with great relief by the population. However, there is always a fly in the ointment, and that was the abolition of the Popular Council.

This latter reform was also greatly resented by powerful sections of the islanders, mainly the aristocracy, the clergy, and the intelligentsia. The temporal power of the Church was slashed in the all-out attempt to concentrate power in the hands of the State. One of these rights which was lost was the immunity from the law enjoyed by anyone, including criminals, who sought refuge in the large number of churches and chapels strewn all over the cities and countryside. The number of churches enjoying such immunity was reduced to a minimum and none could confer any guarantee from immunity against capital punishment. Many country chapels still carry a marble plaque near the front door with the inscription declaring - *Non gode l'immunità ecclesiastica* - 'The Church's immunity is not enjoyed here.' Pius VI confirmed this reform in a *motu proprio*.

In 1783 Sicily suffered greatly from an earthquake and the grand master dispatched the Order's fleet under Balì de Frelon to help the victims. This help was refused because of jealousies that reigned among the various courts of Europe. The fleet distributed clothing, medicines, surgical supplies, and provisions they had on board and returned home.

The effects of the French Revolution were being felt all over Europe. The Order had been existing for some time on the goodwill of some of the more powerful countries. Its own strength and usefulness having been sapped, it seemed, as Bonaparte put it, to have become 'an institution to support in idleness the younger sons of certain privileged families'. In 1772 the French Convention confiscated the rich commanderies of the French langues, which action drastically depleted the resources and further cut down the activities of the Order. But at the same time, it attracted the attention of super-powers to the strategic value of the island. The very auberges were penetrated by revolutionary theories, the main victims being the younger knights.

Rohan was a great reader and kept himself abreast of the progress in science and economics, but he could hardly be expected to entertain any sympathy towards views of such subversive nature as those of the French Revolution. He was himself a Frenchman and an aristocratic one at that, and as such, his sympathies lay with his king and queen. Their survival was very much his concern, although he did his best to remain non-aligned in the struggle going on in France. Yet he managed

Favray: Portrait of Grand Master Emmanuel de Rohan
(National Museum of Fine Arts)

to send some of his golden plate to help pay the expenses of the flight of the royal family.

When the French royal family was arrested and executed, the shock of the news nearly killed Rohan. He fell ill but recovered and lived for another six years. The state of the Order was so low and the feeling of hopelessness amongst the knights was so dominant, that it nearly caused the dissolution of the Order. However, with his usual masterly flair for the grandiose and princely airs, Rohan, just out of his illness, ordered a great religious and civil spectacle. He assembled all the knights in St John's, all dressed in their black hospitaller uniforms, and led them to prayer. He also invited the Maltese to join in the great celebrations, which the islanders did with all the enthusiasm of *festa*-loving people.

This great occasion had the effect it was intended to have; it raised the hopes of knights and islanders in their sovereign and, for a while, all went well. He bestowed his patronage to Żebbug, naming it 'Città Rohan'. The villagers commemorated the event by building a triumphal arch in honour of their beloved 'monarch'. He established the first observatory on the tower of the palace in Valletta and finished the building of the Customs House. He also gave to the city, towards the end of his life, one of its most beautiful and prestigious buildings, the Public Library (today the National Library). To this magnificent building were transferred all the books belonging to the Order, which, by now were considerable since the decree of Lascaris which laid claim for all the books of deceased knights.

Although Rohan was getting old, he was still concerned with the possibility of an attack on the island. Partly because of that, and also to impress foe and friend, he completed the newly-designed Fort Tignè on Dragut Point which guarded the entrance to Marsamxett harbour from the north. Thus he completed the defence of the harbours on either side of Valletta.

De Rohan Arch, Żebbuġ

The beautiful building housing the Public Library – artist's impression

Money was getting extremely scarce yet, through his nature, benign to the last, Rohan changed the rules of recruiting to make it easy for the escaped French nobles to join the Order. The new recruits, penniless, flocked in to live on the finances of the Order. Rohan pleaded with the kings of Spain, Austria, and Portugal for help in the upkeep of these refugees, yet no help was forthcoming. They were all holding to what they had and they certainly were very careful not to be seen antagonizing the revolutionary movement.

The French Republic continued making more and more demands on the Order and kept on making inroads with its revolutionary teachings amongst the French knights, spreading confusion within the brotherhood. No one knew who was for or against

Monument to Grand Master Emmanuel de Rohan

one or the other. To add to the troubles, the British, who were at war with France, made it hard in all ways they could for the Order to carry on. There was only one thing to do: gain alliance or help from a superpower. Rohan despatched Count Litta to St Petersburg asking for Russian protection. Litta was well known in Russia while training naval officers, he had distinguished himself in the Russian navy during Empress Catherine's reign.

Paul I of Russia, who had succeeded his mother Catherine in 1796, received the count with great pomp and promised all the help requested. Revenue to the Order was increased. The czar sent his naval officers to train with the Maltese fleet in preparation for the expansion of his naval forces. Later on, Paul declared himself 'Protector. of the Order' and provided all the needs and cash requested. He solicited for himself and was given the cross of St John of Jerusalem. In return he built a magnificent palace for the ambassador of the Order. A treaty was drawn up between Rohan and Paul but it was never signed as the messenger bearing the papers from St Petersburg to Malta was captured by Napoleon and arrested. The treaty was eventually signed after Rohan's death.

Full of anxiety and foreboding, Rohan fell ill towards the end of 1796 and, on 13 July 1797, he passed away. He was buried in the chapel of France in St John's.

Ferdinand von Hompesch

1797-99

In the hot summer of 1797, the knights elected as Rohan's successor a man who was quite different from his predecessors not only in his nationality, but also in his ways and manners. He was the first German to be elected grand master and the last prince of Malta.

Ferdinand (Joseph Antoine Herman Louis) von Hompesch was born at Bolheim Castle near Dusseldorf on 9 November 1744. At the age of 16, he was engaged as page to Grand Master Pinto. His promotions in the Order were quite spectacular and took place within a very short period. As a very young knight, he was made grand cross and minister of the Order at the court of Vienna where he stayed for 25 years. On his return to Malta, he was appointed balí and head of the langue of Baviere in 1780. He never held any military or naval command yet, as a shrewd diplomat, he ingratiated himself with all around him, people of influence, and the common man. He made a special effort to please the Maltese

Grand Master Ferdinand von Hompesch

by learning to speak their language and by talking to them in the streets. In short, he was a man of superb diplomatic qualities who earned the esteem of all and quick promotions. With the upheaval in France doing away with the monarchy, the Order could hardly entertain the thought of selecting another French master; on the other hand, it was just as unthinkable to elect one with opposing views to the French republicans. It was imperative that a neutral and diplomatic candidate be found. Hompesch was in the right place at the right time. He was elected by a universal vote.

His ingratiation with the people he governed was shown in taking under his special patronage the villages of Żabbar (the inhabitants of Żabbar, in return, built a triumphant arch and called it 'Hompesch Gate'), Żejtun, and Siġġiewi by giving to each, one of his names. Żabbar became 'Città Hompesch' and Siggiewi 'Città Ferdinand', whilst to Żejtun he gave the name of 'Città Beland', after his mother's maiden name.

His very first priority on ascending the throne was to ratify the agreement with Russia in order to secure financial and moral help in view of the darkening horizon of the French Revolution now spreading throughout Europe. France had confiscated the Order's property of the French commanderies and Spain were not going to displease their neighbour, France. The only hope of help was in England, the arch enemy of France, and Russia. Paul I made every effort to please Hompesch and win his favours. Money and gold started coming to the Order through the priory of Poland, now under Russian rule. Hompesch presented Paul with the grand cross of devotion as a symbol of the Order's undying gratitude.

But, at home, the grand master was fast losing his popularity amongst certain knights. The majority of them were French. Their numbers had been increased by refugee knights from the French priory during Rohan's time and they were being kept by

Hompesch Gate

Portrait of Grand Master von Hompesch

the benevolence of the grand master. Others, a few French and many of the Spanish and Italian knights, were reluctant to be involved as they started to see in their leader a flamboyant nature and a superficiality that seemed to overwhelm the man once he had been enthroned. The knights were also annoyed with their grand master giving such consideration to the Maltese people. They resented his way of ingratiating himself with the natives, amongst other things, by distributing coin while he moved amongst them.

To the Maltese common man, there at last was one knight, and the chief one at that, who was prepared to mix with them and speak to them in their own tongue. Differences arose between the two sides and serious scuffles took place at different times and different locations between knights and Maltese. However, French infiltrators and local Francophiles were already hard at work, mostly among the merchants and the Maltese aristocracy, denouncing the autocracy of the Order and highlighting the benefits of equality and the healthy commercial state between Malta and France. But bigger troubles were looming ahead. Napoleon Bonaparte was getting restless: the islands of Malta and Corfu lay right across his plan to conquer Egypt.

In April 1798, at the insistence of Napoleon Bonaparte, the directorate of the French republic issued written orders to Napoleon to capture Malta on his way to Egypt. On 6 June a French squadron of 18 ships under Admiral Brueys was sighted on the horizon. A signal from the French squadron requested that a disabled ship be allowed to enter the harbour for necessary repairs. This request, being made within the treaty of non-alignment, was granted. The crew were allowed ashore while repairs were being carried out. While ashore, contacts were made with sympathizers, both knights and Maltese, to alert them of the imminent arrival of the general and his mighty fleet to occupy the island.

Napoleon Bonaparte

Has history done justice to Hompesch? He is accused of the deliberate betrayal of the institution he was sworn to uphold and protect and of the love and loyalty of the people he accepted to rule. He was irresolute and slow to comprehend the gravity of the situation (after all he was no fighting man). In the confusion he did not trust anyone: all he could imagine was the might of the republic overwhelming his tiny force of 300 knights and about 7,000 fighting men. He is thus pictured by most as the epitome of treachery and cowardice. It could be that, when all the facts are taken into consideration, such verdict appears too harsh and somewhat unfair. Certainly the treachery to the Order came from sources other than Hompesch. It came from the renegade French knights led by the secretary to the treasury appointed by Rohan, Boresdon de Ransijat, who remains as Malta's prime traitor (in fairness to the man, one must record the knight's confession to the magistracy that when he took the oath of the brotherhood he only swore that he would defend the Religion against the infidel Turk and not against his country, Christian France). The few French knights that deserted and the bulk of the Spanish ones who stayed in their auberges ignoring what was going around them, do deserve a fair share of the blame. Hompesch was guilty of weakness and lack of resolution in the face of the inevitable, as no other grand master before him had been. For that he stands fairly condemned of having failed in the face of the enemy because, as he himself admitted, of his ignorance of military discipline and practice.

The sovereignty of the Order of St John of Jerusalem over Malta and its dependencies was over and the Princes of Malta were no more.

Conclusion

On 6 June 1798, a French convoy of 70 ships escorted by two frigates under the command of General Desaix appeared off Marsaxlokk. The following day the general sent a message to the grand master asking him to allow eight French ships to enter harbour to disembark the sick and take on water. Terrified, Hompesch summoned his council. They unanimously refused such a request as it went against the Treaty of 1768 between France, Naples, Spain, and the Order, which only allowed entry to four fighting ships at a time. They expected the general to abide by this treaty. Hompesch was also hoping that his plea for help to the commander-in-chief of the British Mediterranean fleet, Admiral Nelson, stationed in Naples, would be answered in time

On 8 June, 472 ships lay at anchor off Malta with Bonaparte himself on board. Never since the siege of 1565 had Malta seen such a fleet. At 4.30 p.m., Bonaparte approached the island on *L'Orient*. Bonaparte was under instructions from the Revolutionary Council not to jeopardize his main mission, that of capturing Egypt, should Malta offer such resistance as to cause delay and/or to risk engagement with the British navy.

The morning after, the French knight Boresdon de Ransijat, secretary to the treasury and member of Hompesch's war council, declared that his only allegiance was to the French Revolution and called on his co-conspirators to rise against the Order, for which confession of loyalty he was immediately locked in a cell in St Angelo.

Bonaparte, who was informed of the grand master's reply to
Desaix' demand, immediately sent a dispatch to Hompesch
stating his indignation at the insulting refusal to allow some of
his fleet to enter harbour. At the same time, he gave the signal
to his forces to start operations. The French army, 15,000 strong,
landed at St Paul's Bay, Spinola Bay, and Gozo at about 4.00
a.m. of 10 June and captured the whole countryside without
much of a struggle. Some resistance was made at Spinola by a
Maltese regiment and ships of Order sank one frigate These
were, however, easily repulsed and by noon, after a brief
skirmish, most of Malta and Gozo were occupied. A number of
knights joined the French forces under General Vaubois at
Floriana gate, where a Maltese regiment made a rare attack.
Vaubois, seeing the confusion of unseasoned troops, surrounded
them and forced them to retreat behind the fortifications. The
French forces at St Paul's Bay were engaged by a small force of
Maltese militia from Notabile but was totally overrun. The
French forces then marched on Notabile to be greeted at the
open city gates by the nobility who had retired behind the walls
of the old city ever since the Order had set foot on the island,
thus keeping themselves pure in their allegiance towards the
king of Spain. It was not long before they had reason to regret
their action for what they tried to save from destruction by
war, was rapaciously plundered by the same people they
embraced.

The grand master, in consternation, retired to the palace and
failed to give orders, not wanting to take responsibility for the
actions his council might take in the defence of the island.

Confusion reigned supreme. The Maltese garrison at the
Cottonera defences rose against the Order accusing their officers
of betrayal when they found out that the powder was wet and
would not ignite. They killed a number of commanders and
knights. Still Hompesch kept to himself. Some knights, mainly
the loyal French ones, tried to get Hompesch to take a stand

and shoulder his responsibilities and not to dishonour himself and the Order. He was asked to concentrate on defending Valletta, chasing out the collaborators, and insisting with the British fleet to come quickly to their help. The French navy would then, they hoped, sail away. But Hompesch remained silent.

The French started their approach on Valletta. A detachment of the Maltese garrison repulsed the first attack but had to retreat under the onslaught of a larger force of more experienced fighters. The fighting carried on into the night when confusion amongst the Maltese broke out. By midnight, a deputation of Maltese notables had an audience with Hompesch and told him that, if the will to fight was not in him, he ought to capitulate and avoid a bloodbath and the massacre of knights and Maltese. Hompesch refused, still hoping that the British navy would arrive in time. The delegation then sent word to Bonaparte offering him the city at a given signal. The deputation again approached Hompesch asking him to surrender. He then called the council and finally decided to ask for an armistice. Some historians state that Hompesch still believed that the sovereignty of the Order over Malta was not in question.

A French delegation, made up of Junot, ADC to Bonaparte, Commander Dolomieu (who was the French contact of Ransijat), and M. Poussiegle, was sent to the grand master to arrange the cease fire.

It was agreed that the grand master send a deputation within 24 hours to sign the capitulation. And so the French flag replaced that of the Order and Malta now came under French rule.

The Articles of Capitulation were:

1. The knights of the Order of St John of Jerusalem will surrender the city and the forts of Malta to the French Army.

They renounce all the rights of sovereignty to all property they have, were they in the city or on the islands of Malta, Gozo, or Comino, in favour of the French Army.

2. The French Republic will use its influence at the congress of Rastadt to obtain for the lifetime of the grand master a principality equal to that he is losing and, in the meantime, it pledges itself to grant him an annual pension of 300,000 francs. Besides this, he will receive a sum equal to two years of such a pension as indemnity for his furniture. He will retain all military honours he enjoyed until such time as he will remain in Malta.

3. The French knights in Malta, the state of whom will be decided by the general-in-chief, could return to their country and their residence in Malta would be reckoned as residence in France.

4. The French Republic will award a life pension of 700 francs to the French knights at present in Malta. This pension will be 1,000 francs for sexagenarian knights. The French Republic will use its good offices with the Cisalpine, Ligurian, Roman, and Swiss Republics so that the present article be conveyed to the knights of these different nations.

5. The French Republic will use its good offices with the other European powers so that they will concede to the knights of their nationality the exercise of their rights on the property of the Order of Malta situated in their States.

6. The knights will retain their property on the islands of Malta and Gozo as their private property.

7. The inhabitants of the islands of Malta and Gozo will continue to enjoy as in the past, the free practice of the Catholic, Apostolic, Roman Religion. They will retain the

property and privileges they possess; no extraordinary contribution will be imposed.

8. All past civil acts under the government of the Order will be valid and will be enforced.

Done in duplicate on the ship *L'Orient* off Malta on 24th priorial, sixth year of the French Republic (old style - 12 June 1798).

Signed Bonaparte.

Commander Bosredon Ransijat, Barone Mario Testaferrata, Dottore G. Nicole Muscat, Dottore Benedetto Schembri, Balì di Toria (sic for Torino) Frisani, Cabellero Filipe de Amati.

In consequence the following dispositions were then arranged:

Article 1: Today the 24 priorial, Fort Manoel, Fort Tignè, the Castle of St Angelo, the fortifications of Bormola, Cottonera, and the city of Vittoriosa to be handed to the French troops at midday.

Article 2: Tomorrow, the 25 priorial, Fort Ricasoli, the Castle of St Elmo, the fortifications of the city of Valletta, those of Floriana, and all the others will be handed over to the French troops by midday.

Article 3: French officers will go today at 10.00 o'clock in the morning to the grand master, in order to convey the instructions to the governor in charge of the forts and fortifications which are to be handed over to the French; they will be accompanied by a Maltese officer. There will be as many officers as there are forts to be consigned.

Article 4: The same dispositions as above will be followed for the forts and fortifications which are to be consigned to the French tomorrow on the 25 priorial.

Article 5: Artillery, depots, and strategic papers will be handed over together with the fortifications.

Article 6: The troops of the Order of Malta may remain in the barracks they now occupy until further notice.

Article 7: The admiral-in-chief of the French fleet will appoint an officer to take over today's vessels, galleys, warships, depots, and other naval auxiliaries belonging to the Order.

signed:
Bonaparte

Barth di Toriol (sic for Torino) Evisari, Commander Bosredan Ransijat, Barone Mario Testaferrata, Dottore G. Nicole Muscat, Dottore Benedetto Schembri, Cabellero Filipe de Amati.

(From Ermel de Wismes, *Les Chevaliers de Malte*).

Bonaparte landed on Malta without éven paying a visit to the grand master who, after passing through all the degrees of humiliation, would yet stand this last one. He decided to go himself to Bonaparte accompanied by his knights. He was well received, but Bonaparte did not accede to any of his requests. On the contrary the knights were ordered to leave the island within a limited time.

A sovereign Order with a glorious history of seven centuries was crushed and annihilated in a few hours by the infamous weakness of an incompetent and weak grand master and the corruption and treachery of the French knights. The knights then found themselves in an embarrassing situation and they scattered throughout Europe.

Two days after the interview with Bonaparte, Hompesch wrote a letter to the French general, the terms of which he afterwards denied. Hompesch sailed away from Malta, abandoning the Order's archives, his knights, and the treasures of the Order on the island. Thirty-four days later he arrived in Trieste. Forty-two French knights found themselves in a situation which could not but lead them to follow their master and, on 19 June, the French fleet took some knights away to Trieste, where Hompesch still pretended to be grand master. Before leaving Malta, the grand master asked for and obtained permission to take with him the miraculous image of Our Lady of Philermos, together with a piece of the True Cross.

Pius VI issued a brief against Hompesch who was not prepared to abdicate. A number of the abandoned knights fled to Russia where they were reunited in the grand priory of St Petersburg under the protection of Paul I of Russia. Paul, protector of the Order, saw his opportunity for the magistracy which would be for him a means of acquiring Malta. Making use of the pope's brief condemning Hompesch's action by pretending the brief was intended for him as a sign to claim the magistracy, he opened negotiations on the subject through the court of Vienna to force Hompesch to abdicate in his favour. Some historians claim that Hompesch finished by giving in, and left Trieste to await further developments residing successively at Neustadt, Gortstadt, Porta di Fumo, and Città di Castello, always ignored by his family for his infamy regarding Malta. Other knights made their way to the Vatican, repudiating Hompesch and his magistracy and advising Pius VI on the vacancy and the election of a successor.

However, Hompesch did not give up the fight and tried and

tried again and again to be re-established in his former dignity, but his efforts were in vain. He finally settled in Montpellier (France) where he died on 12 May 1805. The fight for succession to the magistracy continued between the Vatican and the Russian throne, the situation to-date being: a total break between the two arms of the Venerable Order of Knights (Hospitaller and Militant) of St John of Jerusalem, and, worse still, the two charitable camps vying with each other for, and claiming, the right of succession. Humanity never learns the adage: Divided .....

Bibliography

Blouet, Brian, *The Story of Malta* (London, 1972).

Boisgelin, Louis de, *Ancient and Modern Malta* (London, 1805).

Bradford, Ernle, *The Great Siege of Malta, 1565* (London, 1961).

Caruana, A., *Storia ta Malta* (Malta, 1904).

Cassar, Paul, *Medical History of Malta* (Malta, 1966).

Cousins, J.D., *The Siege of St Elmo* (Malta, 1952).

Cavaliero, Roderick, *The Last of the Crusaders* (London, 1960).

De Bono, P., Judge, *History of Malta* (Malta, 1803).

Gauci, G., *Il Grande Assedio di Malta* (Malta, 1891).

Laferla, A.V., *The Story of Man in Malta* (Malta 1935).

Luke, Sir Harry, *Malta - An Account and an Appreciation* (London, 1949).

Schermerhorn, E.W., *Malta of the Knights* (London, 1929).

Scicluna, Sir Hannibal, *The Church of St John in Valletta* (Rome, 1955).

Smith, Harrison, *Order of St John of Jerusalem* (Malta, 1961, revised by J. Storace).

Tonna-Barthet, Gaston, *Bibliography of the Grand Masters of the Sovereign Order of St John of Jerusalem* (Jerusalem, 1974).

Vassallo, G.A., *Storia di Malta* (Malta,1848).

Vella, Andrew, *The University of Malta* (Malta, 1964).

Zammit, Sir Themistocles, *Malta. The Islands and their History* (Malta, 1926).